LONGMAN

THE TOEFL® TEST

COMPUTER
TEST
OVERVIEW

DEBORAH PHILLIPS

Longman

longman.com

Longman Prepare for the TOEFL® Test: Computer Test Overview
(This book was originally published under the title Longman
Preparation Course for the TOEFL® Test: CBT Volume.)

Copyright © 2003 by Pearson Education, Inc.

Pearson Education, 10 Bank Street, White Plains, NY 10606

Vice president, instructional design: Allen Ascher
Senior acquisitions editor: Virginia Blanford
Vice president, director of design and production: Rhea Banker
Executive managing editor: Linda Moser
Production editor: Michael Mone
Production coordinator: Melissa Leyva
Director of manufacturing: Patrice Fraccio
Manufacturing supervisor: Edie Pullman
Project editors: Helen B. Ambrosio, Lisa Hutchins
Text design adaptation: Page Designs
Text composition: Paula D. Williams
Text illustration: Lloyd Birmingham, Jill C. Wood
Text photography: Richard Hutchings, Hutchings Photography
Cover design: Ann France
Additional art credits appear on page 179.

Library of Congress Cataloging-in-Publication Data

Phillips, Deborah
    Longman Prepare for the TOEFL® Test: Computer Test Overview /
    Phillips, Deborah.
        p. cm.
    ISBN: 0-13-111666-5
    1. Test of English as a Foreign Language—Study guides.
2. English language—Textbooks for foreign speakers. 3. English
language—Examinations—Study guides. I. Title.
PE1128.P4615 2003
428'.0076—dc21   98-43066
                                CIP

ISBN: 0-13-110765-8 (Book/CD ROM/Audio CDs package)
Printed in the United States of America
1 2 3 4 5 6 7 8 9 10–BAH–05 04 03 02 01 00

Contents _____

Introduction

About Longman Prepare for the TOEFL® Test: Computer Test Overview

Longman is proud to be one of the world's leading publishers of preparation materials for the TOEFL® test. Most of the books that Longman publishes, including the *Longman Complete Course for the TOEFL® Test* and the *Longman Introductory Course for the TOEFL® Test*, are designed to be used primarily in classroom preparation courses. This package, however—*Longman Prepare for the TOEFL® Test: Computer Test Overview*—is specifically designed for you. This program can be used in brief overview preparation courses, but it is also the perfect combination for self-study, to prepare you to take the TOEFL Computer-Based Test (CBT). The components in this package are based on the most up-to-date information available on the format and style of the TOEFL CBT.

For individual test-takers, this program provides:

- An introductory overview of the strategies and skills needed for the TOEFL Computer-Based Test for students taking the test for the first time.

- A wealth of additional practice opportunities for students who are already familiar with the TOEFL CBT and want more review, or for first-time test-takers who want to become more familiar with the format and style of the test.

For classroom-based instruction, this program can be used as:

- The primary text in a short course intended to provide students with basic strategies and skills practice in preparation for the TOEFL CBT.

- A supplementary text in a more general ESL/EFL course, to familiarize students with the TOEFL CBT.

Longman Prepare for the TOEFL® Test: Computer Test Overview consists of a book, two audio CDs, and a computer CD-ROM (the *Longman Student CD-ROM*). These three components are all essential pieces of a complete preparation program for the TOEFL Computer-Based Test.

What Will You Find In This Book?

The *Longman Prepare for the TOEFL® Test: Computer Test Overview* includes the perfect combination of materials for students who want an overview of the exam and ample practice opportunities or a chance to review and measure what they already know. What does it include?

- **Examples with Explanations** for each type of question appearing on the TOEFL CBT guide you through the process of answering every kind of TOEFL test item.

- **Test-Taking Strategies** for each of the sections on the TOEFL CBT provide you with clearly defined steps to improve your performance on the test.

- Extensive **Exercises** for each section on the TOEFL CBT allow you to practice every type of question using the suggested strategies.

- The **Writing Skills Section** provides you with the writing skills necessary to improve your performance on the Writing section of the TOEFL CBT.

- **Listening Scripts** provide transcriptions of all of the listening exercises included on the audio CDs that accompany the book.

- An **Answer Key** allows you to check your own answers against the correct ones.

- **Diagnostic Charts** relate the questions in the book to the language practiced on the *Longman Student CD-ROM* that accompanies this book.

What Will You Find on the Audio CDs?

The two audio CDs in this package contain recordings of all the listening comprehension exercises and tests in the *Longman Prepare for the TOEFL® Test: Computer Test Overview* book.

Audio CD 1		
• **The Short Dialogues**	text pages 3-12	CD tracks 1-35
• **The Casual Conversations**	text pages 13-19	CD tracks 36-45
• **The Academic Discussions**	text pages 20-33	CD tracks 46-49
Audio CD 2		
• **The Academic Lectures**	text pages 34-46	CD tracks 1-4
• **Practice Test**	text pages 47-54	CD tracks 5-19

What Will You Find on the *Longman Student CD-ROM*?

The CD-ROM included here is the *Longman Student CD-ROM* (the same CD-ROM that is included with the *Longman Complete Course for the TOEFL® Test*). This CD-ROM offers extensive opportunities for practice and skill-building to prepare you for the challenges of the TOEFL CBT—over 1500 TOEFL-format questions and 200 additional writing practice questions.

- **A Tutorial** demonstrates how to answer each type of question found on the TOEFL Computer-Based Test.

- **Practice Questions** for each of the sections on the TOEFL CBT—a total of over 800 items—provide you with the opportunity to master each of the language skills and types of questions on the test.

- An additional 900 questions comprise **Section Tests** and **Complete Tests** that simulate the actual testing conditions—including timing, adaptivity, and format—of the TOEFL CBT and allow you to measure your progress under real test conditions.

- **Explanations** for all test items help you understand your errors and learn from your mistakes.

- **Scoring and Record-Keeping functions** enable you to monitor your progress.

- **Screens, Buttons, and Clicking Sequences** similar to those on the TOEFL CBT provide you with practice that simulates actual test conditions.

The *Longman Student CD-ROM* contains practice exercises, section tests, and complete tests. The results of these exercises and tests are recorded within the computer program and may also be printed and kept in a notebook. The practice exercises can be used in two different ways:

(1) they can be completed systematically from start to finish, or
(2) they can be used to review specific skills that have been identified as requiring further practice.

The chart below describes the content of the *Longman Student CD-ROM*. (See the *How to Use This Kit* booklet for definitions of these skills.)

The LONGMAN STUDENT CD-ROM

LISTENING PRACTICE

Short Dialogues

- *Skills 1-3*   10 questions
- *Skills 4-6*   10 questions
- *Skills 7-10*   10 questions
- *Skills 11-13*   10 questions
- *Skills 14-15*   10 questions
- *Skills 16-17*   10 questions

Casual Conversations

- *Conversations 1*   8 questions
- *Conversations 2*   8 questions
- *Conversations 3*   8 questions
- *Conversations 4*   8 questions
- *Conversations 5*   8 questions

Academic Discussions

- *Discussion 1*   5 questions
- *Discussion 2*   5 questions
- *Discussion 3*   5 questions
- *Discussion 4*   5 questions

Academic Lectures

- *Lecture 1*   5 questions
- *Lecture 2*   5 questions
- *Lecture 3*   6 questions
- *Lecture 4*   6 questions
- *Lecture 5*   6 questions

STRUCTURE PRACTICE

Structure

- *Skills 1-5*   20 questions
- *Skills 6-8*   20 questions
- *Skills 9-12*   20 questions

- *Skills 13-14*   20 questions
- *Skills 15-19*   20 questions

Written Expression

- *Skills 20-23*   20 questions
- *Skills 24-26*   20 questions
- *Skills 27-29*   20 questions
- *Skills 30-32*   20 questions
- *Skills 33-36*   20 questions
- *Skills 37-38*   20 questions

- *Skills 39-42*   20 questions
- *Skills 43-45*   20 questions
- *Skills 46-48*   20 questions
- *Skills 49-51*   20 questions
- *Skills 56-57*   20 questions
- *Skills 58-60*   20 questions

READING PRACTICE

Easy Passages

- *Passage 1*   11 questions
- *Passage 2*   11 questions
- *Passage 3*   12 questions

Medium Passages

- *Passage 1*   12 questions
- *Passage 2*   11 questions
- *Passage 3*   12 questions

Difficult Passages

- *Passage 1*   11 questions
- *Passage 2*   12 questions
- *Passage 3*   11 questions

WRITING PRACTICE

Before and While Writing

- *Before and While Writing 1*   25 questions
- *Before and While Writing 2*   25 questions
- *Before and While Writing 3*   25 questions

After Writing

Editing Sentence Structure   20 questions
Inversions and Agreement
Parallel, Comparative, and
    Superlative Structures   20 questions
Nouns and Pronouns   20 questions
Adjectives and Adverbs   20 questions
Prepositions and Usuage   20 questions

INDIVIDUAL SECTION TESTS

Listening Tests

- *Listening Test One*   30 questions
- *Listening Test Two*   30 questions
- *Listening Test Three*   50 questions

STRUCTURE TESTS

Reading Tests

Tests in an adaptive base   200 questions

- *Reading Test One*   44 questions
- *Reading Test Two*   44 questions
- *Reading Test Three*   60 questions

Writing Tests

Questions in a base   18 questions

COMPLETE TESTS

- Complete TOEFL Test One   100 questions*
- Complete TOEFL Test Two   130 questions*

*The Complete Test Structure questions come from a separate adaptive base of 200 questions. **In a classroom setting**, the section tests and complete tests can be used periodically as diagnostic pre-tests before the material is introduced in the book, midway through the preparation program to assess progress, or as post-tests to measure results.

What Other TOEFL Preparation Materials Are Available From Longman?

For more comprehensive preparation for both the computer-based and the paper-based TOEFL tests, you may want to explore the following Longman products:

- The *Longman Complete Course for the TOEFL® Test*, which provides comprehensive coverage of the language skills and test-taking strategies for both the TOEFL CBT and the TOEFL paper-based test, including exercises, diagnostic pre-tests, post-tests, and complete practice tests in the format of both the paper and the computer tests. To use this book, you will also need to purchase the audio program that accompanies it.

- The *Longman Introductory Course for the TOEFL® Test,* which, together with the audio program that accompanies it, provides intermediate students with the skills, strategies, practice, and confidence they need to increase their scores on all sections of the TOEFL test in both computer and paper formats.

- The *Longman Preparation Course for the TOEFL® Test: Practice Tests*, which offers five complete tests that reproduce the format and style of the TOEFL paper-based test.

For more information about these Longman products, please visit **www.longman.com**.

About the TOEFL Computer-Based Test

What Is the TOEFL CBT?

The TOEFL Computer-Based Test (CBT) is designed to measure the level of English proficiency of non-native speakers of English. It is required primarily by English-language colleges and universities. Additionally, institutions such as government agencies, businesses, or scholarship programs may require this test.

The TOEFL CBT has the following sections:

- **Listening:** To demonstrate their ability to understand spoken English, examinees must first listen to passages on headphones as they see pictures on a computer screen and then answer various types of questions about the passages that they just heard.

• **Structure:** To demonstrate their ability to recognize grammatically correct English, examinees must look at sentences on a computer screen and either choose the correct way to complete the sentences or identify errors in the sentences.

• **Reading:** To demonstrate their ability to understand written English, examinees must read passages on a computer screen and answer various types of questions about the meanings of words and ideas in the passages.

• **Writing:** To demonstrate their ability to produce meaningful and correct written English, examinees must write an essay on a given topic in thirty minutes, either on the computer or by hand.

The typical TOEFL CBT follows this format:

Listening	30-50 questions	40-60 minutes
Structure	20-25 questions	15-20 minutes
Reading	44-60 questions	70-90 minutes
Writing	1 essay	30 minutes

How Do I Register for the TOEFL Computer-Based Test?

You should plan to register for the TOEFL CBT at least four weeks before you hope to take it to increase your chances of being able to take the test when and where you prefer. You should follow these steps to register for the TOEFL Computer-Based Test:

• Obtain a copy of the *TOEFL® Bulletin*. You can obtain the *TOEFL® Bulletin* by ordering it or downloading it from the TOEFL website at www.toefl.org, by calling 1-609-771-7100, or by mailing a request to the following address:

TOEFL Services
Educational Testing Service
P.O. Box 6151
Princeton, NJ 08541-6151 USA

• Use the *TOEFL® Bulletin* to determine where the most convenient computer test centers are located. You may be asked to suggest more than one test center, so you should identify two or more convenient centers before you register.

• Follow the procedures listed in the *TOEFL® Bulletin* for registering for the test. You may register for the test either by phone or by mail. The phone numbers and addresses for registering from different parts of the world are listed in the *TOEFL® Bulletin*.

Keep in mind that you may *take* the TOEFL CBT more than once, but you may *register* for it only once per calendar month. If you take the test more than once within a calendar month, you will not receive the new scores and you will not receive a refund on your test fee.

How is the TOEFL Computer-Based Test Scored?

The TOEFL CBT is scored on a scale of 0 to 300 points. There is no official passing score on this test. Instead, individual institutions have their own score requirements. You must find out from each institution what score is required. The following chart shows how the scores on the TOEFL Computer-Based Test are related to the scores on the paper-and-pencil test:

Paper TOEFL® Test	Computer TOEFL® Test
677	300
650	280
600	250
550	213
500	173
450	133
400	97
350	63
300	40

You need to understand the scoring of the TOEFL CBT before you take the test because you will be asked to make decisions about scoring at the end of the test. At the end of the test, the following will happen:

- You will be asked whether or not you want to cancel the score. If a score is cancelled at this point, it cannot be reinstated at a later date.

- You will be shown your score range for the test that you have just taken. This score range is based on the listening, structure, and reading questions that you answered but does not include the essay score.

- You will be asked whether your official score should be sent to the institutions designated in the test application. You must judge from the score range, your writing ability, and the scores required by the institutions whether or not to send the scores at this point. If you decide not to send the score reports at this point, you may send them later for an additional fee.

Scores are mailed out approximately two weeks after the test date to examinees who type their essays. Scores are mailed out approximately five weeks after the test date to examinees who write their essays by hand.

How Should I Prepare for Taking the TOEFL CBT?

The TOEFL Computer-Based Test is a test of English. However, your score will be better if you are also adept at taking tests and if you are familiar with the format and requirements of this specific test, including the computer aspects of it. To do well on this test, you should focus on three different areas:

- Your knowledge of English language skills.
- Your mastery of test-taking strategies specific to the TOEFL CBT.
- Your familiarity with the basic computer skills needed on the TOEFL CBT.

This book—*Longman Prepare for the TOEFL® Test: Computer Test Overview*—provides an overview of the test and will familiarize you with the best strategies for taking it. The *Longman Student CD-ROM* included in this package gives you extensive practice with the item types, allows you to simulate the conditions of a real test, and familiarizes you with the necessary computer skills.

However, strategies, computer skills, and even extensive practice are only a part of the preparation process for the TOEFL CBT. Your basic language skills in English must also be strong. For a comprehensive preparation course in English language skills as tested on the TOEFL CBT, we recommend the *Longman Complete Course for the TOEFL® Test* and its accompanying audio program.

Developing a Study Plan

A good place to start when preparing for the TOEFL Computer-Based Test is to study each of the types of questions in this book. Pay careful attention to the strategies recommended for each type of question.

- As you work through the book, pay attention to the language skills that are being tested. (The language skills being tested in the questions in each exercise are noted in parentheses in the answer key on pages 163–168 at the back of this book and are listed in the booklet, *How to Use This Kit*.)

- As you identify the language skills that are difficult for you, practice these language skills in the practice section of the *Longman Student CD-ROM*.

- When you feel comfortable with your ability to answer the different types of questions in each section, complete the sample test at the end of that section.

- Complete the diagnostic charts on pages 175–178 at the back of the book. What language skills are still causing you problems? Continue to practice those skills, both in the exercises in the book and in the section tests on the CD-ROM.

- Periodically, as you prepare, complete the test sections on the *Student CD-ROM*. Taking test sections on the *Student CD-ROM* allows you to simulate the actual testing conditions of the TOEFL CBT and to measure your progress.

If you design an effective self-study program and give yourself enough time to complete it, you should be able to achieve the TOEFL CBT score you want.

Good luck!

THE LISTENING SECTION

The first section of the TOEFL® Computer-Based Test is the Listening section. In this section, you will listen to recorded material, look at visual cues, and respond to questions about the material. You must listen carefully because you will hear the recorded material one time only and the recorded material does not appear on the computer screen.

Four types of passages may appear in the Listening section of the TOEFL® Computer-Based Test:

1. A **Short Dialogue** consists of a two-to-four line dialogue between two speakers. Each Short Dialogue is accompanied by a context-setting visual and is followed by one question.
2. A **Casual Conversation** consists of a five-to-seven line conversation on a casual topic. Each Casual Conversation is accompanied by a context-setting visual and is followed by two or three questions.
3. An **Academic Discussion** consists of a 120-to-150 second discussion on an academic topic by two to five speakers. Each discussion is accompanied by a number of context-setting visuals and is followed by three to six questions.
4. An **Academic Lecture** consists of a 120-to-150 second lecture on an academic topic by a university professor. Each lecture is accompanied by a number of context-setting visuals and is followed by three to six questions.

This section of the test begins with the short dialogues. The remaining questions in this section of the test consist of a mixture of the other three types of listening passages.

GENERAL STRATEGIES

1. **Be familiar with the directions.** The directions on every TOEFL® Computer-Based Test are the same, so it is not necessary to spend time reading the directions carefully when you take the test. You should be completely familiar with the directions before the day of the test.

2. **Be familiar with computer adaptivity.** This section of the TOEFL® Computer-Based Test is adaptive. This means that you will start with a medium-level question, and the difficulty of the questions will increase or decrease depending on whether or not your answers are correct.

3. **Set the volume carefully before you start the Listening section.** You have the opportunity to set the volume before you start the section.

4. **Dismiss the directions as soon as they come up.** The timer starts when the directions come up. You should already be familiar with the directions. Then you can hit `Dismiss Directions` as soon as it appears and save all your time for the questions.

5. **Listen carefully to the spoken material.** You will hear the spoken material one time only. You may not repeat the spoken material during the test.

6. **Use the visuals to help you focus on the context.** As you listen to the spoken material, you will see visual materials on the screen. The visual information may help you to understand the context for the spoken material as you listen.

7. **Pace yourself between questions.** You control when the spoken material is played. You may take as much time as you need between questions.

8. **Think carefully about a question before you answer it.** You may not return to a question later in the test to change the answer. You have only one opportunity to answer a given question.

9. **Answer each question as it comes up on the screen.** You may not choose to skip or omit any of the questions. You must answer each one.

10. **Do not spend too much time on a question you are unsure of.** If you truly do not know the answer to a question, simply guess and go on. The computer will automatically move you into a level of questions that you can answer.

11. **Be very careful not to make careless mistakes.** If you mistakenly choose an incorrect answer, the computer will move you to an easier level of questions than you can handle. You will have to waste time working your way back to the appropriate level of questions.

12. **Monitor the time and the number of questions carefully on the title bar of the computer screen.** The title bar indicates the time remaining in the Listening section, the total number of questions in the section, and the current number.

13. **Do not randomly guess at the end of the section to complete all the questions in the section before time is up.** In a computer adaptive section such as listening, random guessing to complete the section will only lower your score.

THE SHORT DIALOGUES

For each of the Short Dialogues in the Listening section of the TOEFL® Computer-Based Test, you will see a context-setting visual as you listen to a two-to-four line dialogue between two speakers. After you see the visual and listen to the dialogue, you will see the question and the four answer choices on the computer screen. You must click on the best answer choice on the computer screen, click on **Next**, and then click on **Confirm Answer**.

Example

You see on the computer screen: You hear:

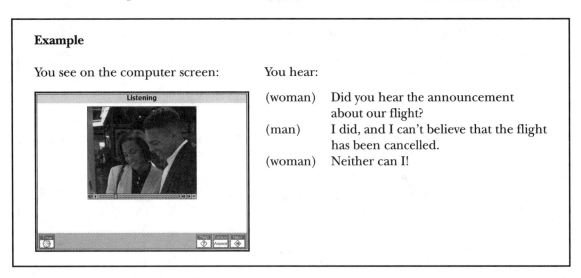

(woman)   Did you hear the announcement about our flight?
(man)   I did, and I can't believe that the flight has been cancelled.
(woman)   Neither can I!

After the dialogue is complete, the question and answer choices appear on the computer screen as the narrator states the question. This question is a regular multiple choice question that asks what the woman means.

You see on the computer screen: You hear:

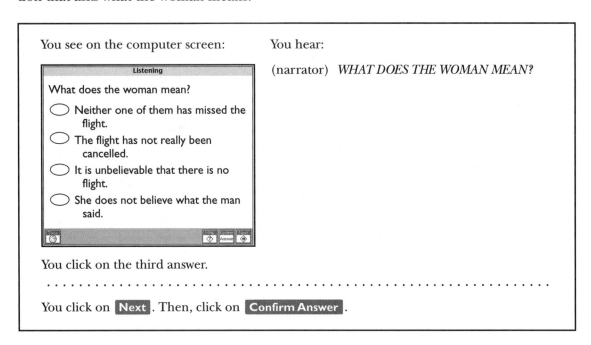

(narrator)   *WHAT DOES THE WOMAN MEAN?*

You click on the third answer.

· ·

You click on **Next**. Then, click on **Confirm Answer**.

In the dialogue, the woman says *neither can I* to indicate that she agrees with the man. The man *can't believe that the flight was cancelled,* so the woman also thinks that it is *unbelievable that there is no flight.* The third answer is therefore the best answer to this question. You should click on the third answer, click on Next , and then click on Confirm Answer to record your answer.

STRATEGIES FOR THE SHORT DIALOGUES

1. **Listen carefully to the short dialogue.** You may listen to the dialogue one time only.

2. **Use the visual to help you focus on the context.** A visual appears on the screen at the beginning of each short dialogue. It shows you who is talking and where they are talking.

3. **As you listen to each short conversation, focus on the last line of the dialogue.** The answer to the question is generally found in the last line of the dialogue.

4. **Listen to the question following the short dialogue as you read it on the screen.** Each listening question is both spoken and written on the computer screen.

5. **Keep in mind that the correct answer is probably a restatement of a key word or idea in the last line of the dialogue.** Think of possible restatements of the last line of the dialogue.

6. **Keep in mind that certain structures and expressions are tested regularly in the dialogues.** Listen for these structures and expressions:
   - structures (*passives, negatives, wishes, conditions*)
   - functional expressions (*agreement, uncertainty, suggestion, surprise*)
   - idiomatic expressions (*two-part verbs, three-part verbs, proverbs*)

7. **Even if you do not understand the complete dialogue, you can find the correct answer.**
   - If you only understood a few words or ideas in the last line, choose the answer that contains a restatement of those words or ideas.
   - If you did not understand anything at all in the last line of the dialogue, choose the answer that sounds the most different from what you heard.
   - Never choose an answer because it *sounds like* what you heard in the dialogue.

8. **Click on an answer on the computer screen when you have selected an answer.** You may still change your mind at this point and click on a different answer.

9. **Click on Next . Then, click on Confirm Answer to record your answer.** After you click on this button, you cannot go back and change your answer.

10. **Be prepared for the next question.** After you click on Confirm Answer , the next question begins automatically.

Diagnostic Pre-Test: SHORT DIALOGUES

The Diagnostic Pre-Test includes the language skills that will be tested in the Short Dialogues questions on the TOEFL® Computer-Based Test. You can use the Pre-Test to determine which skills require further work. Then you can practice each of these language skills on the Student CD-ROM. (Each of the language skills tested here is presented comprehensively in the *Longman Complete Course for the TOEFL® Test*.)

DIRECTIONS: Look at the picture as you listen to each short dialogue. Do not look at the questions or answer choices until the dialogue is complete. (On the TOEFL® Computer-Based Test, you will not be able to see the questions or answer choices during the dialogue.)

1. What does the woman mean?
   ○ The show was unbelievable.
   ○ She didn't see all of the show.
   ○ She doesn't believe that the show really happened.
   ○ The skydivers were pulled off their feet.

2. What should the man do?
   ○ Step around the building and enter through the first door
   ○ Go through the first door and go down the steps
   ○ Go down the hall and enter the doorway
   ○ Descend the stairs and go in the second door

3. What does the man mean?
   ○ The laundry is getting done.
   ○ They are close to the cleaners.
   ○ The woman should close the machine.
   ○ He is watching someone clear the machine.

4. Who are these people most likely to be?
   - ○ Construction workers
   - ○ Architects
   - ○ Insurance agents
   - ○ Artists

5. What does the man mean?
   - ○ The landlord has raised the rent.
   - ○ The landlord has received a letter with some bad news.
   - ○ The landlord will not increase the rent.
   - ○ The landlord will not rent them an apartment.

6. What does the woman mean?
   - ○ She convinced Jack to go.
   - ○ She will not be able to go to the restaurant.
   - ○ Jack has convinced her to go to a restaurant.
   - ○ Jack is not going.

7. What does the man say about the weather?
   - ○ It is quite humid this week.
   - ○ The humidity will last through the week.
   - ○ It is drier now.
   - ○ It was better just last week.

8. What does the man mean?
   - ○ He was not surprised by the change.
   - ○ He didn't expect the change.
   - ○ The requirements have not changed.
   - ○ He expects to change his major.

9. What does the woman mean?

   ◯ They were unable to pay the bill.
   ◯ The prices were surprisingly low.
   ◯ The restaurant was too expensive for them to try.
   ◯ They almost didn't have enough to pay for the meal.

10. What does the woman mean?

   ◯ The trip was less than perfect.
   ◯ There was nothing at all wrong with the trip.
   ◯ There wasn't any way that she could take the trip.
   ◯ The trip could have been improved in a number of ways.

11. What does the woman mean?

   ◯ She would like the man to repeat himself.
   ◯ The last exam was not very hard.
   ◯ She agrees with the man about the exam.
   ◯ The man has repeated himself several times.

12. What does the woman suggest?

   ◯ Leaving on Tuesday
   ◯ Cutting their visit short
   ◯ Changing the day of their departure
   ◯ Postponing their visit to a later date

13. What had the man assumed?

   ◯ That she would take the course
   ◯ That the first lecture would not be tomorrow
   ◯ That he would not be in the course
   ◯ That she would not register

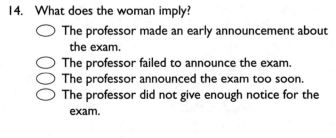

14. What does the woman imply?
- ◯ The professor made an early announcement about the exam.
- ◯ The professor failed to announce the exam.
- ◯ The professor announced the exam too soon.
- ◯ The professor did not give enough notice for the exam.

15. What does the man imply?
- ◯ The runner did not fall.
- ◯ The team won.
- ◯ The loss was the runner's fault.
- ◯ The team won't ever win a game.

16. What does the man say about the room?
- ◯ It has probably not been arranged.
- ◯ It is ready for the conference.
- ◯ It needs a set of chairs.
- ◯ It needs to be emptied.

17. What does the woman mean?
- ◯ The bridge is too hard to cross.
- ◯ They can decide later.
- ◯ They must pay rent for the bridge.
- ◯ They must cross a bridge to get to the house.

Check your answers in the Answer Key on page 163.
Then turn to page 175 and circle the numbers of the questions that you missed.

Post-Test: SHORT DIALOGUES

The Post-Test includes the language skills that will be tested in the Short Dialogues questions on the TOEFL® Computer-Based Test. You can use the Post-Test to measure your proficiency after you have completed the related sections on the Student CD-ROM.

DIRECTIONS: Look at the drawing as you listen to each short dialogue. Do not look at the questions or answer choices until the dialogue is complete. (On the TOEFL® Computer-Based Test, you will not be able to see the questions or answer choices during the dialogue.)

1. What does the man say about the results?
   - ◯ They are unconfirmed.
   - ◯ They are dependent on future research.
   - ◯ They are most probably correct.
   - ◯ They are independent of the researchers' ideas.

2. What does the man want to do?
   - ◯ Go out now
   - ◯ Enjoy the rest of the evening
   - ◯ Have a little snack before going out
   - ◯ Take a short nap

3. What does the man mean?
   - ◯ It's a good idea to be thrifty.
   - ◯ He's feeling a little dirty.
   - ◯ He'd like something to drink.
   - ◯ Stopping for thirty minutes is a good idea.

4. What is the woman probably doing?

    ◯ Visiting a doctor
    ◯ Attending a reception
    ◯ Interviewing for a job
    ◯ Applying to medical school

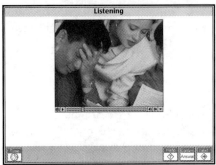

5. What does the woman mean?

    ◯ The lawyer delivered the letter this morning.
    ◯ The courier has already made the delivery.
    ◯ The letter to the courier has already been received.
    ◯ The lawyer's office does not have the letter.

6. What does the man say about Cathy?

    ◯ She must work tonight.
    ◯ The shift in her plans is unlucky.
    ◯ Her roommate is persuasive.
    ◯ Her roommate will work in her place.

7. What does the man imply about the report?

    ◯ It is not done yet.
    ◯ It contains a lot of errors.
    ◯ It was not done carelessly.
    ◯ It does not seem to have been done by the accountant.

8. What does the woman think?

    ◯ That the man should not reach out so far
    ◯ That the man can accomplish what he wants
    ◯ That the man will be unable to graduate
    ◯ That the man cannot score a goal

9. What does the man mean?
- ◯ He has never gone to any games.
- ◯ It is rare for the football team to win.
- ◯ He doesn't go to games often.
- ◯ It is rare for the university team to have a game.

10. How did Anna feel about the situation?
- ◯ She was less than delighted.
- ◯ She was quite pleased.
- ◯ She was unable to accept it.
- ◯ She wished she could have been more delighted.

11. What does the man mean?
- ◯ He's going to say something in the theater.
- ◯ What the woman said was magnified out of proportion.
- ◯ The size of the theater was magnificent.
- ◯ He shares the woman's opinion.

12. What does the woman suggest?
- ◯ Going home on the bus
- ◯ Sleeping on the bus
- ◯ Taking a quick walk
- ◯ Getting some sleep before going home

13. What had the woman assumed about Tom?
- ◯ That he would be at work
- ◯ That he knew a lot about architecture
- ◯ That he did not get the job
- ◯ That he would not be at home

14. What does the man imply?
  ◯ He has to take microbiology.
  ◯ He wishes he could take microbiology this semester.
  ◯ He had hoped to take microbiology this semester.
  ◯ He is not enrolling in microbiology this semester.

15. What does the woman imply?
  ◯ She couldn't afford a new computer.
  ◯ The computers were not on sale.
  ◯ She was unable to get a new computer.
  ◯ She bought a new computer.

16. What does the woman ask the man to do with the cigarette?
  ◯ Put it away
  ◯ Put it off
  ◯ Put it out
  ◯ Put it down

17. What does the man mean?
  ◯ He thinks the assignment will take about two hours.
  ◯ He cannot work on the assignment because of a headache.
  ◯ It would be better to prepare two assignments than one.
  ◯ He prefers not to work on it by himself.

Check your answers in the Answer Key on page 163.
Then turn to page 175 and circle the numbers of the questions that you missed.

THE CASUAL CONVERSATIONS

For each of the Casual Conversations in the Listening section of the TOEFL® Computer-Based Test, you will see a context-setting visual as you listen to a five-to-seven line conversation between two speakers. After you see the visual and listen to the conversation, you will see a series of two or three questions and the four answer choices for each question on the computer screen. You must click on the best answer choice to each question on the computer screen, click on [Next], and then click on [Confirm Answer].

Example

You see on the computer screen:

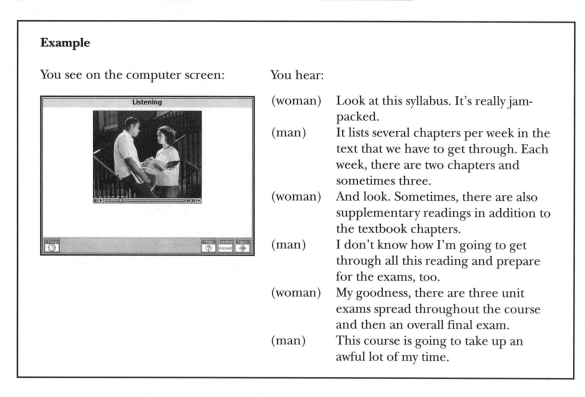

You hear:

(woman)	Look at this syllabus. It's really jam-packed.
(man)	It lists several chapters per week in the text that we have to get through. Each week, there are two chapters and sometimes three.
(woman)	And look. Sometimes, there are also supplementary readings in addition to the textbook chapters.
(man)	I don't know how I'm going to get through all this reading and prepare for the exams, too.
(woman)	My goodness, there are three unit exams spread throughout the course and then an overall final exam.
(man)	This course is going to take up an awful lot of my time.

After the conversation is complete, the first question and answer choices appear on the computer screen as the narrator states the question. This question is a regular multiple choice question that asks about the *weekly reading assignments*.

You see on the computer screen:

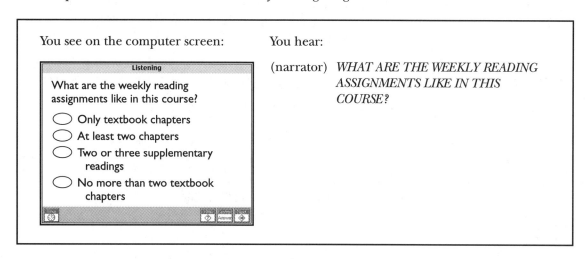

You hear:

(narrator) *WHAT ARE THE WEEKLY READING ASSIGNMENTS LIKE IN THIS COURSE?*

You click on the second answer.

. . . .

You click on Next . Then, click on Confirm Answer .

The man states in the dialogue that there are ...*several chapters per week...two chapters and some-times three,* and the woman states that ...*sometimes there are also supplementary readings.* Because there are *at least two chapters* every week, the second answer is the best answer to this question. You should click on the second answer, click on Next , and then click on Confirm Answer to proceed to the next question.

After you have clicked on Confirm Answer , another question and answer choices appear on the computer screen as the narrator states the question. This question asks about the number of *total exams.*

You see on the computer screen: You hear:

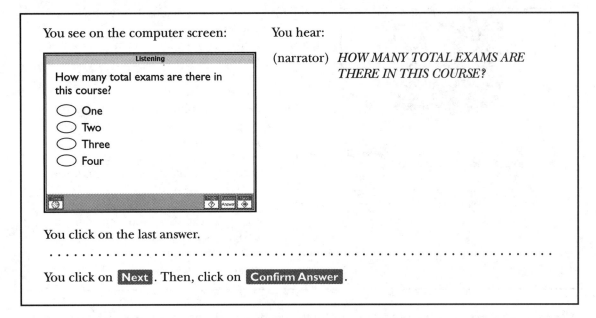

(narrator) *HOW MANY TOTAL EXAMS ARE THERE IN THIS COURSE?*

You click on the last answer.

. . . .

You click on Next . Then, click on Confirm Answer .

The woman states that ...*there are three unit exams spread throughout the course and then an overall final exam.* Because there are three unit exams and one overall final exam, the total number of exams is four. The last answer is therefore the best answer to this question. You should click on the last answer, click on Next , and then click on Confirm Answer to proceed to the next passage.

STRATEGIES FOR THE CASUAL CONVERSATIONS

1. **Listen carefully to the casual conversation.** You may listen to the conversation one time only.

2. **Use the visual to help you focus on the context.** The visual appears on the screen at the beginning of each casual conversation. It shows you who is talking and where they are talking.

3. **Focus on the overall meaning of the casual conversation rather than on specific words or expressions.** The questions following a casual conversation generally test your overall comprehension of the conversation rather than the meaning of a specific word or expression.

4. **Listen to each question following the casual conversation as you read it on the screen.** Each listening question is both spoken and written on the computer screen.

5. **Do not panic if you do not understand all of the details of the casual conversation.** You can still answer the questions correctly without understanding each detail of the conversation.

6. **Click on an answer on the computer screen when you have selected an answer.** You may still change your mind at this point and click on a different answer.

7. **Click on** Next **and then click on** Confirm Answer **to record your answer.** After you click on this button, you cannot go back and change your answer.

8. **Be prepared for the next question.** After you click on Confirm Answer, the next question begins automatically.

Exercise: CASUAL CONVERSATIONS

DIRECTIONS: Look at the picture as you listen to each casual conversation. Do not look at the questions or answer choices until the conversation is complete. (On the TOEFL® Computer-Based Test, you will not be able to see the questions or answer choices during the conversation.)

Questions 1-2

1. What problem does the man have?
   ◯ He can't find a map.
   ◯ He can't find a building.
   ◯ He can't find the campus.
   ◯ He can't find the corner.

2. What is true about Henderson Hall?
   ◯ It is a modern building.
   ◯ It is a tall building.
   ◯ It was one of the first university buildings.
   ◯ It is on the other side of campus.

Questions 3-4

3. What is included in the study abroad program?
    ○ A semester of study at the university and a
       semester break in Italy
    ○ A semester of study in Italy
    ○ A two-week trip to Italy during the semester
    ○ A two-semester program, one at the university and
       one in Italy

4. Why isn't the woman taking part in the study abroad
    program?
    ○ It sounds like a terrible program.
    ○ She's not an art major.
    ○ She doesn't really care for Italian art.
    ○ She doesn't have the money needed for the
       program.

Questions 5-6

5. When is the woman's next class?
    ○ An hour after the man's
    ○ In half an hour
    ○ An hour and a half later than the man's
    ○ Before the man's

6. What will the students probably do next?
    ○ Make some coffee
    ○ Hurry to their next classes
    ○ Spend half an hour getting to the student center
    ○ Head over to meet some people

Questions 7-9

7. Who is Dr. Benjamin?
    ⃝ A doctor at the university medical center
    ⃝ An employee of the Environmental Protection
        Agency
    ⃝ A well-known lecturer
    ⃝ An actor at the university theater

8. What is mentioned about Dr. Benjamin's talks?
    ⃝ They are given in the local area around the
        university.
    ⃝ They are about the environment at the university.
    ⃝ They are required for students in the
        Environmental Studies Department.
    ⃝ They are not intended solely for the university.

9. What will the woman probably do?
    ⃝ Get a new calendar
    ⃝ Miss the opportunity to talk to Dr. Benjamin
    ⃝ Take part in a theater production
    ⃝ Attend a lecture on the environment

Questions 10-11

10. What was mentioned about the dance production?
    ⃝ It was a professional production.
    ⃝ The dancers were from the department.
    ⃝ It was two hours long.
    ⃝ It took two weeks to prepare.

11. How did the woman feel about the performance?
    ⃝ There were no problems in the performances.
    ⃝ The dancers were not really prepared.
    ⃝ The dance style was too classical.
    ⃝ She would have preferred something more modern.

Questions 12-14

12. Why can't the man play tennis today?
    ○ He will be busy preparing a schedule.
    ○ He has other plans.
    ○ He is spending six hours in the library.
    ○ He only plays tennis first thing in the morning.

13. How might the man's life be described?
    ○ Meticulously organized
    ○ Full of sports activities
    ○ Loosely planned
    ○ Lacking in accomplishment

14. What does the woman say about her life?
    ○ She schedules every minute of every day.
    ○ She will stick to her plan to play tennis.
    ○ She probably isn't as productive as the man.
    ○ She certainly isn't as disorganized as the man.

Questions 15-16

15. What can be inferred about pass/fail grading in this department?
    ○ It is used in the advanced courses.
    ○ A grade of seventy is not passing.
    ○ A student with a very high grade gets a grade of A.
    ○ It is used in five out of seven courses.

16. What is indicated about the grading in the department?
    ○ All courses are graded in the same way.
    ○ Advanced courses have pass/fail grading.
    ○ The introductory course has letter grading.
    ○ There won't be grades such as A or B in the introductory course.

Questions 17-18

17. Why is the presentation important?
    ○ Its overall grade is the course grade.
    ○ It is in only two weeks.
    ○ It is an important part of the course grade.
    ○ It is half an hour long.

18. How much have the two students prepared up to now?
    ○ They have prepared half the presentation.
    ○ They have worked on the presentation a lot in the last two weeks.
    ○ They have practiced the presentation only one time.
    ○ They have only planned their strategies for the presentation.

Questions 19-20

19. What will happen with the econometrics course next semester?
    ○ It will have morning and evening sections.
    ○ It will have three sections.
    ○ It will have a section from 7:00 to 10:00 in the morning.
    ○ It will have evening sections on Monday, Wednesday, and Friday.

20. What is true about the man?
    ○ He describes himself as a morning person.
    ○ He is not going to take econometrics.
    ○ He is planning to take a course that meets three times per week.
    ○ He will be in the Tuesday course.

Check your answers in the Answer Key on page 163.
Then turn to page 175 and circle the numbers of the questions that you missed.

THE ACADEMIC DISCUSSIONS

For each of the Academic Discussions in the Listening section of the TOEFL® Computer-Based Test, you will see a series of context-setting visuals as you listen to a 120-to-150 second discussion by two-to-five speakers. After you see the visuals and listen to the discussion, you will hear a series of questions as you see each question and its answer choices on the computer screen. You must click on the best answer choice to each question on the computer screen, click on Next , and then click on Confirm Answer .

A variety of types of questions are possible in this part of the test. Some of these types of questions may follow a discussion:

- a multiple choice question with one correct answer
- a multiple choice question with two correct answers
- a matching question
- an ordering question
- a question with four graphic answer choices
- a question and a graphic with four letters marked

The following example of a discussion shows each of these types of questions. On the actual TOEFL® Computer-Based Test, you will probably not see all of these types of questions accompanying one discussion.

Example

You see on the computer screen:

You hear:

(narrator) *LISTEN TO A GROUP OF STUDENTS DISCUSSING INFORMATION FROM A HISTORY CLASS. THE DISCUSSION IS ON THE HISTORY OF THE STATUE OF LIBERTY.*

(man 1) ❶ First, let's review the historical background of the Statue of Liberty.

(woman) Good idea. There's going to be a quiz on Friday, and that's one of the topics on Friday's quiz.

(man 2) The Statue of Liberty is on an island in upper New York Bay. What was the name of the island?

(man 1) The island used to be known as Bedloe's Island because a man named Isaac Bedloe had owned the island in the seventeenth century. The name was officially changed to Liberty Island in 1956.

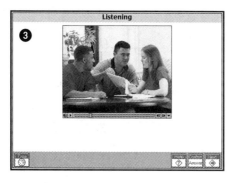

(woman)	In the early nineteenth century, a military fort was built on the island to defend New York against military attack. The fort was named Fort Wood, in honor of military hero Eleazar Wood.
(man 2)	So the island was named Bedloe's Island, and the fort on the island was named Fort Wood?
(woman)	Exactly. The fort is a star-shaped construction in the middle of the island. The pedestal of the statue was constructed to rise out of the middle of the star-shaped Fort Wood. ❷ You can see this in the picture in our textbook.
(man)	I believe that the Statue of Liberty was a gift to the American people from the French. The idea for a joint French–American monument to celebrate liberty was proposed, and an organization was established to raise funds and oversee the project.
(woman)	The statue itself was a gift from the French, but the project was more of a joint French–American project. A total of $400,000 was donated by the French people to build the statue, and the American people raised the funds to build the pedestal on which it stands.
(man 2)	And it was a French sculptor who designed the statue? Who was he?
(man 1)	French sculptor Frederic Auguste Bartholdi designed the statue and also oversaw its construction. Did you know that he designed the face of the statue to look like his mother?
(woman)	No, I didn't. That's interesting. The Statue of Liberty has the face of Bartholdi's mother.
(man 1)	❸ When was the statue constructed?
(man 2)	Construction on the statue began in 1875 in Paris. Bartholdi had wanted to have the statue completed for the United States' 1876 centennial celebration, but this turned out to be impossible.
(woman)	But by the time of the centennial celebration in 1876, the right hand and torch had been completed. This part of the statue was sent to the United States for display at centennial celebrations in Philadelphia and New

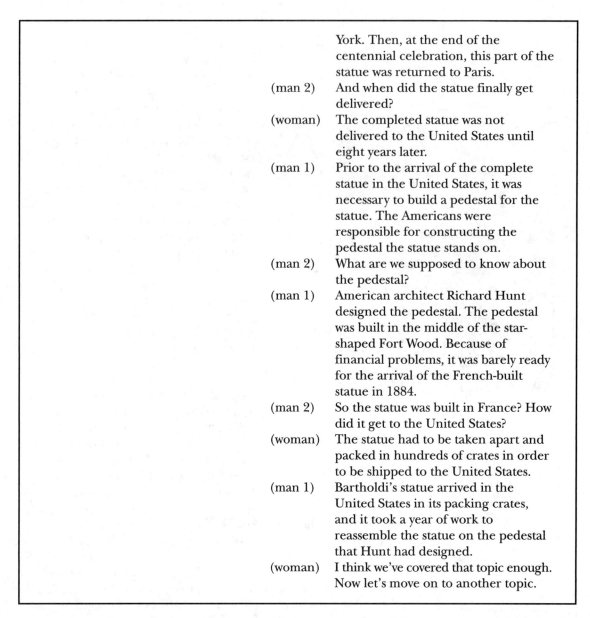

(man 2)	York. Then, at the end of the centennial celebration, this part of the statue was returned to Paris.
(man 2)	And when did the statue finally get delivered?
(woman)	The completed statue was not delivered to the United States until eight years later.
(man 1)	Prior to the arrival of the complete statue in the United States, it was necessary to build a pedestal for the statue. The Americans were responsible for constructing the pedestal the statue stands on.
(man 2)	What are we supposed to know about the pedestal?
(man 1)	American architect Richard Hunt designed the pedestal. The pedestal was built in the middle of the star-shaped Fort Wood. Because of financial problems, it was barely ready for the arrival of the French-built statue in 1884.
(man 2)	So the statue was built in France? How did it get to the United States?
(woman)	The statue had to be taken apart and packed in hundreds of crates in order to be shipped to the United States.
(man 1)	Bartholdi's statue arrived in the United States in its packing crates, and it took a year of work to reassemble the statue on the pedestal that Hunt had designed.
(woman)	I think we've covered that topic enough. Now let's move on to another topic.

After the discussion is complete, the first question and answer choices appear on the computer screen as the narrator states the question. This question is a regular multiple choice question that asks what the students are preparing for.

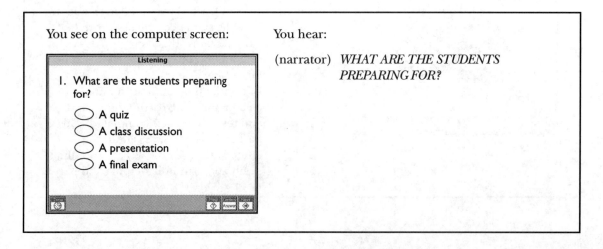

You see on the computer screen:

Listening

1. What are the students preparing for?

○ A quiz
○ A class discussion
○ A presentation
○ A final exam

You hear:

(narrator) *WHAT ARE THE STUDENTS PREPARING FOR?*

You click on the first answer.

. . . .

You click on Next . Then, click on Confirm Answer .

In the discussion, the woman mentions *a quiz on Friday*. You should click on the first answer because the first answer is the best answer to this question. You need to click on Next and then click on Confirm Answer to proceed to the next question.

After you have clicked on Confirm Answer , another question and answer choices appear on the computer screen as the narrator states the question. This question is an example of a multiple choice question with two possible answers.

You see on the computer screen: You hear:

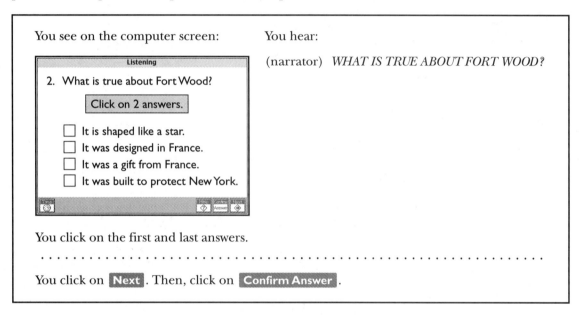

(narrator) *WHAT IS TRUE ABOUT FORT WOOD?*

You click on the first and last answers.

. . . .

You click on Next . Then, click on Confirm Answer .

In the discussion, the woman says that the *fort was built on the island to defend New York against military attack* and that the *fort is a star shaped construction*. This means that the fort *is shaped like a star* and that it was *built to protect New York*. The first and last answers are therefore the best answers to this quesiton. You need to click on Next and then click on Confirm Answer to proceed to the next question.

After you have clicked on Confirm Answer , a third question and answer choices appear on the computer screen as the narrator states the question. This question is a matching question about what each person did.

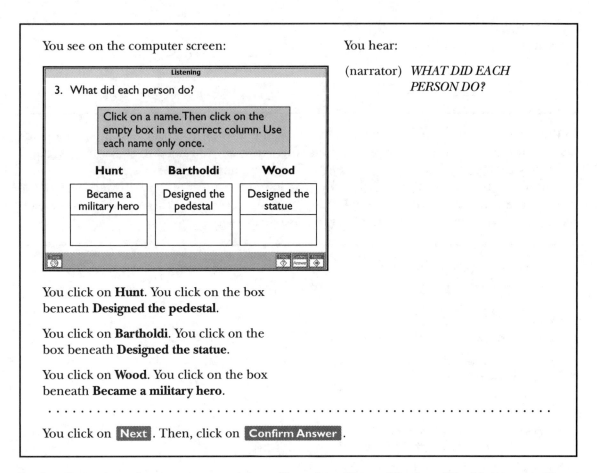

You see on the computer screen:

You hear:

(narrator) *WHAT DID EACH PERSON DO?*

You click on **Hunt**. You click on the box beneath **Designed the pedestal**.

You click on **Bartholdi**. You click on the box beneath **Designed the statue**.

You click on **Wood**. You click on the box beneath **Became a military hero**.

You click on Next . Then, click on Confirm Answer .

In the discussion, the woman mentions *military hero Eleazar Wood*, so *Wood became a military hero*. The first man mentions that *French sculptor Frederic Auguste Bartholdi designed the statue,* so *Bartholdi designed the statue*. The first man later mentions that *American architect Richard Hunt designed the pedestal,* so *Hunt designed the pedestal*. You need to click on Next and then click on Confirm Answer to proceed to the next question.

After you have clicked on Confirm Answer , a fourth question and answer choices appear on the computer screen as the narrator states the question. This question is an ordering question about a historical series of events.

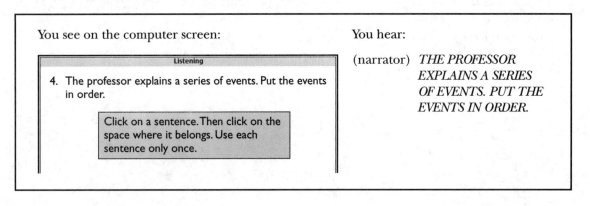

You see on the computer screen:

You hear:

(narrator) *THE PROFESSOR EXPLAINS A SERIES OF EVENTS. PUT THE EVENTS IN ORDER.*

The American centennial took place.

The construction of the statue was begun.

The statue was completely assembled in New York.

Part of the statue was returned to Paris.

1 _____

2 _____

3 _____

4 _____

You click on **The construction of the statue was begun.** You click on the first box.

You click on **The American centennial took place.** You click on the second box.

You click on **Part of the statue was returned to Paris.** You click on the third box.

You click on **The statue was completely assembled in New York.** You click on the last box.

. . . .

You click on Next . Then, click on Confirm Answer .

In the passage, it is stated that *construction of the statue began in 1875,* that *the centennial celebration was in 1876,* that *at the end of the celebration this part of the statue was returned to Paris,* that *the arrival of the French-built statue was in 1884,* and that *it took a year of work to reassemble the statue.* From this, it can be determined that first the construction of the statue was begun, then the American centennial took place, then part of the statue was returned to Paris, and finally the statue was completely assembled in New York. You need to click on Next and then click on Confirm Answer to proceed to the next question.

After you have clicked on Confirm Answer , a fifth question and answer choices appear on the computer screen as the narrator states the question. This question asks you to click on one of four pictures to indicate which part of the statue arrived first from France.

You see on the computer screen:

You hear:

(narrator) *WHICH PART OF THE*
STATUE ARRIVED FIRST
FROM FRANCE?

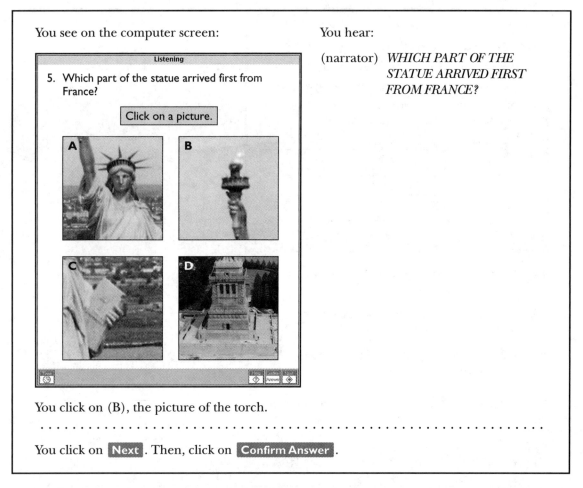

You click on (B), the picture of the torch.

· ·

You click on Next . Then, click on Confirm Answer .

In the discussion, the woman says that *by the time of the centennial celebration in 1876, the right hand and torch had been completed* and that *this part of the statue was sent to the United States for display.* From this it can be inferred that the *right hand and torch* arrived first from France. You need to click on Next and then click on Confirm Answer to proceed to the next question.

After you have clicked on Confirm Answer , a sixth question and answer choices appear on the computer screen as the narrator states the question. This question asks you to click on one of four letters on a map to identify the island that used to be called Bedloe's.

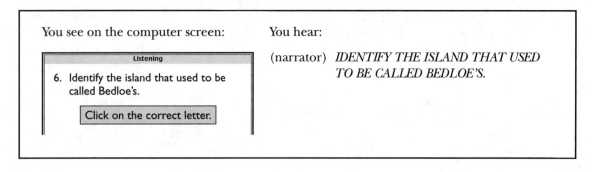

You see on the computer screen:

You hear:

(narrator) *IDENTIFY THE ISLAND THAT USED*
TO BE CALLED BEDLOE'S.

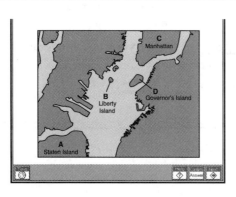

You click on (B), Liberty Island.

. . . .

You click on **Next** . Then, click on **Confirm Answer** .

In the discussion, the first man states that *the island used to be known as Bedloe's Island* and that *the name was officially changed to Liberty Island.* From this, it can be determined that Liberty Island used to be called Bedloe's Island. You need to click on **Next** and then click on **Confirm Answer** to proceed to the next passage.

STRATEGIES FOR THE ACADEMIC DISCUSSIONS

1. **Listen carefully to the academic discussion.** You may listen to the discussion one time only.

2. **Use the first visual to help you focus on the context.** The first visual appears on the screen at the beginning of each academic discussion. It shows you how many people are talking and where they are talking. Anywhere from two to five people could be taking part in an academic discussion.

3. **Focus on the overall meaning of the academic discussion rather than on specific words or expressions.** The questions following an academic discussion generally test your overall comprehension of the discussion rather than the meaning of a specific word or expression.

4. **Relate the remaining visuals to the academic discussion.** The remaining visuals are related to the portion of the discussion that you hear as you see the visual.

5. **Listen to each question following the academic discussion as you read it on the screen.** Each question is both spoken and written on the computer screen.

6. **Understand the ordering of questions that accompany an academic discussion.** The answers to the questions that accompany a discussion are generally found in order in the discussion. The answer to the first question will generally be found closer to the beginning of the discussion, and the answer to the last question will generally be found closer to the end of the discussion.

7. **Do not panic if you do not understand all of the details of the academic discussion.** You can still answer the questions correctly without understanding each detail of the discussion.

8. **Click on an answer on the computer screen when you have selected an answer.** You may still change your mind at this point and click on a different answer.

9. **Click on** Next **and then click on** Confirm Answer **to record your answer.** After you click on this button, you cannot go back and change your answer.

10. **Be prepared for the next question.** After you click on Confirm Answer , the next question begins automatically.

Exercise: ACADEMIC DISCUSSIONS

DIRECTIONS: Look at the pictures as you listen to each academic discussion. Move from picture to picture when you hear a beep on the tape. Do not look at the questions or answer choices until the lecture is complete. (On the TOEFL® Computer-Based Test, you will not be able to see the questions or answer choices during the lecture.)

Questions 1-5

Listen as an instructor leads a discussion of some material from a psychology class. The class was on sleep.

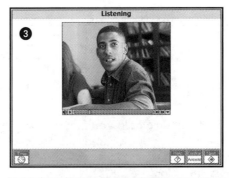

1. What happens during human sleep?
    ○ Muscles tense.
    ○ The rate of breathing increases.
    ○ The heart rate decreases.
    ○ Brain waves flatten.

2. What types of brain wave activity are common during human sleep?

    Click on 2 answers.

    ☐ Short, fast brain waves
    ☐ Short, slow brain waves
    ☐ Long, fast brain waves
    ☐ Long, slow brain waves

3. Identify the animal that probably has changes in brain wave activity during sleep but does not dream.

    Click on a picture.

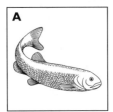 A
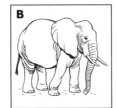 B
 C
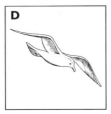 D

4. How long are the periods of dreaming for each of these animals?

    Click on a word. Then click on the empty box in the correct column. Use each word only once.

fish	mammals	birds
No periods of dreaming	Brief periods of dreaming	Longer periods of dreaming

5. Identify the part of the brain wave pattern when dreaming takes place.

    Click on the correct letter.

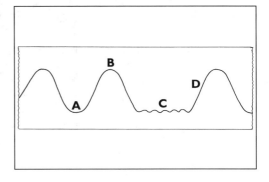

Questions 6-10

Listen to a group of students discussing a report for a history class. The report is on the history of eyeglasses.

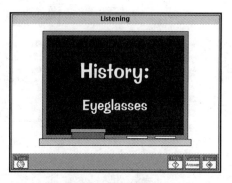

6. How long are eyeglasses known to have been in use?
   ◯ Since 1720
   ◯ For more than seven hundred years
   ◯ Since the seventeenth century
   ◯ For more than twelve hundred years

7. What are the various types of eye pieces?

   Click on the name of an eye piece. Then click on the empty box in the correct column. Use each name only once.

monocle	lorgnette	prospect glass
Has a long handle	Looks like a telescope	Covers one eye

8. Select the eye piece that would most likely have been used by a ninetheenth-century woman.

   Click on a picture.

   A 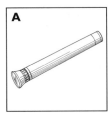 B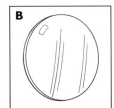
   C  D

9. The students discuss a series of historical events. Put the events in order.

   Click on a sentence. Then click on the space where it belongs. Use each sentence one time only.

   Monocles were fashionable.
   The first eyeglasses were invented.
   Framed eyeglasses became fashionable.
   Prospect glasses were fashionable.

   1 _____
   2 _____
   3 _____
   4 _____

10. How do the speakers compare the older versions of eyeglasses to today's eyeglasses?
    ◯ They were more fashionable than today's glasses.
    ◯ They were easier to use than today's glasses.
    ◯ They were less convenient than today's glasses.
    ◯ They were more comfortable than today's glasses.

Questions 11-15

Listen to a group of students discussing some material from an oceanography lecture. The lecture was on changes in sea level.

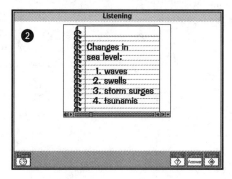

11. When do the students have this conversation?

○ Before class
○ After reading a textbook chapter
○ While studying for an exam
○ After a lecture

12. Identify the wave that is most probably a swell.

Click on a picture.

13. What is true about storm surges?

Click on 2 answers.

☐ They result from changes in pressure ahead of a storm.
☐ They most often occur close to shore.
☐ They start on the ocean floor.
☐ They are also known as tidal waves.

14. What is the cause of each of these changes in sea level?

Click on an expression. Then click on the empty box in the correct column. Use each expression only once.

tsunamis	storm surges	waves
Caused by surface wind	Caused by low pressure	Caused by earthquakes

15. The students describe the process of a storm surge. Summarize the process by putting the events in order.

Click on a sentence. Then click on the space where it belongs. Use each sentence one time only.

The surge hits the coastline.

Flooding ensues.

Low pressure and winds cause a storm.

The winds push water ahead of the storm.

1	
2	
3	
4	

Check your answers in the Answer Key on page 163.
Then turn to page 175 and circle the numbers of the questions that you missed.

THE ACADEMIC LECTURES

For each of the Academic Lectures in the Listening section of the TOEFL® Computer-Based Test, you will see a series of context-setting visuals as you hear a 120-to-150 second lecture by a university professor. After you see the visuals and listen to the lecture, you will hear a series of questions as you see each question and its answer choices on the computer screen. You must click on the best answer choice to each question on the computer screen, click on Next , and then click on Confirm Answer .

A variety of types of questions are possible in this part of the test. Some of these types of questions may follow a lecture:

- a multiple choice question with one correct answer
- a multiple choice question with two correct answers
- a matching question
- an ordering question
- a question with four graphic answer choices
- a question and a graphic with four letters marked

The following example of a lecture shows each of these types of questions. On the actual TOEFL® Computer-Based Test, you will probably not see all of these types of questions accompanying one lecture.

Example

You see on the computer screen:

You hear:

LISTEN TO A LECTURE IN A BIOLOGY CLASS. THE PROFESSOR IS TALKING ABOUT FOOD CHAINS.

❶ A food chain refers to the process in nature by which animals are fed by other animals and plants. All animals are ultimately dependent on plants for food: some animals eat plants directly, while other animals eat animals that eat plants. In this way, food chains develop.

A simple food chain consists of one producer, one primary consumer, and one secondary consumer. ❷ Look at this diagram of a simple food chain. In such a food chain, a producer is always a plant, and that plant is eaten by a primary consumer, which is a plant-eating animal called a herbivore. The primary consumer is eaten by a secondary consumer, a meat-eating animal called a carnivore. An example of a simple food chain would start with grass, which is eaten by a rabbit, which is then eaten by a fox.

A more complicated food chain can have more than one secondary consumer, or carnivore. In this type of food chain, one meat-eating carnivore devours the plant-eating herbivore, and another meat-eating carnivore devours the first meat-eating carnivore. ❸ Look at this example of a more complicated food chain. This example begins with grasses, which are eaten by the plant-eating antelope. At the next stage of the food chain, the antelope is eaten by the carnivorous lion, which then can be devoured by a second carnivore in the food chain, such as a vulture. There cannot be more than one producer in a complicated food chain because one plant does not eat another, and there cannot be more than one primary consumer because one plant-eating animal does not eat another plant-eating animal. However, a food chain can have a number of secondary consumers, carnivores that feast on lower animals in the food chain.

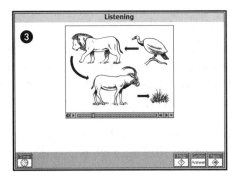

A further complication to some food chains is that one animal can enter the food chain at various stages. This means that one animal can enter a food chain as either a primary consumer, a herbivore, or as a secondary consumer, a carnivore. ❹ Now we will look at an example of a food chain in which one of the animals enters the food chain twice. This food chain begins with grasses which can be eaten by the plant-eating rabbit. A baboon can be part of this food chain as either a primary or a secondary consumer. As a primary consumer, it feeds on the grasses, and as a secondary consumer, it feeds on the rabbit. A leopard can also be part of this food chain as a secondary consumer that feeds on the baboon.

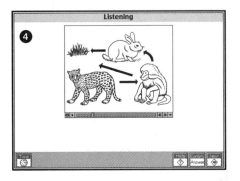

After the discussion is complete, the first question and answer choices appear on the computer screen as the narrator states the question. This question is a regular multiple choice question that asks about a simple food chain.

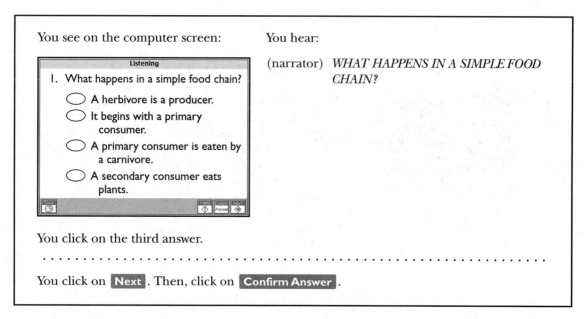

You see on the computer screen:

You hear:

(narrator) *WHAT HAPPENS IN A SIMPLE FOOD CHAIN?*

You click on the third answer.

. . . .

You click on Next . Then, click on Confirm Answer .

In the lecture, the professor states that *the primary consumer is eaten by a secondary consumer, a meat-eating animal called a carnivore.* This means that *a primary consumer is eaten by a carnivore.* You should click on the third answer because the third answer is the best answer to the quesiton. You need to click on Next and then click on Confirm Answer to proceed to the next question.

After you have clicked on Confirm Answer , another question and answer choices appear on the computer screen as the narrator states the question. This question is a multiple choice question with two correct answers.

You see on the computer screen:

You hear:

Listening

2. What happens in a complicated food chain?

Click on 2 answers.

☐ There may be more than one secondary consumer.
☐ There is only one producer.
☐ A herbivore may be a secondary consumer.
☐ A primary consumer is a carnivore.

(narrator) *WHAT HAPPENS IN A COMPLICATED FOOD CHAIN?*

You click on the first and second answers.

. . . .

You click on Next . Then, click on Confirm Answer .

This question asks about a complicated food chain. In the lecture, the professor states that *a more complicated food chain can have more than one secondary consumer* and that *there cannot be more than one producer in a complicated food chain*. This means that *there may be more than one secondary consumer* and that *there is only one producer*. You should click on the first and second answers because these are the best answers to this question. You need to click on **Next** and then click on **Confirm Answer** to proceed to the next question.

After you have clicked on **Confirm Answer**, a third question and answer choices appear on the computer screen as the narrator states the question. This question is a matching question about the components of a food chain.

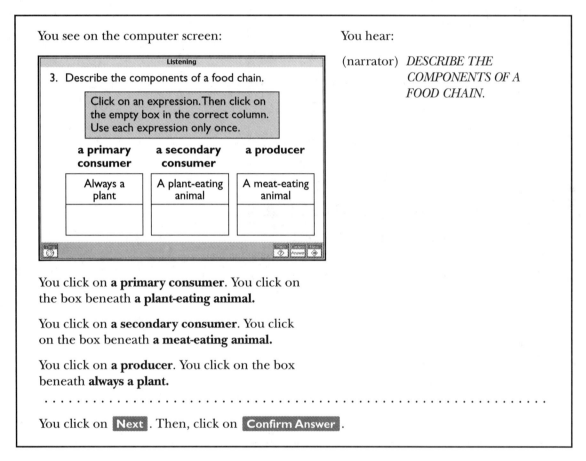

You see on the computer screen:

You hear:

(narrator) *DESCRIBE THE COMPONENTS OF A FOOD CHAIN.*

You click on **a primary consumer.** You click on the box beneath **a plant-eating animal.**

You click on **a secondary consumer.** You click on the box beneath **a meat-eating animal.**

You click on **a producer.** You click on the box beneath **always a plant.**

· ·

You click on **Next**. Then, click on **Confirm Answer**.

In the lecture, the professor states that *a producer is always a plant..., a primary consumer...is a plant-eating animal...*, and *a secondary consumer is a meat-eating animal. A producer* therefore matches up with *always a plant, a primary consumer* matches up with *a plant-eating animal,* and *a secondary consumer* matches up with *a meat-eating animal.* You need to click on **Next** and then click on **Confirm Answer** to proceed to the next question.

After you have clicked on **Confirm Answer**, a fourth question and answer choices appear on the computer screen as the narrator states the question. This question is an ordering question about the process of a food chain.

You see on the computer screen:

You hear:

Listening

4. The professor explains a process. Summarize the process by putting the events in order.

> Click on a sentence. Then click on the space where it belongs. Use each sentence only once.

A carnivore eats a primary consumer.
A producer grows.
One secondary consumer eats another.
A herbivore eats a plant.

1 [   ]

2 [   ]

3 [   ]

4 [   ]

(narrator) *THE PROFESSOR EXPLAINS A PROCESS. SUMMARIZE THE PROCESS BY PUTTING THE EVENTS IN ORDER.*

You click on **A producer grows.** You click on the first box.

You click on **A herbivore eats a plant.** You click on the second box.

You click on **A carnivore eats the primary consumer.** You click on the third box.

You click on **One secondary consumer eats another.** You click on the fourth box.

. . . .

You click on [Next]. Then, click on [Confirm Answer].

In the lecture, the professor states that *a producer is always a plant, and that plant is eaten by a primary consumer, which is a plant-eating animal called a herbivore. The primary consumer is eaten by a secondary consumer, a meat-eating animal called a carnivore.* The professor later explains that *in a more complicated food chain…, another meat-eating carnivore devours the first meat-eating carnivore.* From this it can be determined that first a producer grows, then a herbivore eats a plant, then a carnivore eats a primary consumer, and finally one secondary consumer eats another. You need to click on [Next] and then click on [Confirm Answer] to proceed to the next question.

After you have clicked on [Confirm Answer], a fifth question and answer choices appear on the computer screen as the narrator states the question. This question asks you to click on one of four pictures to indicate which one could be a herbivore.

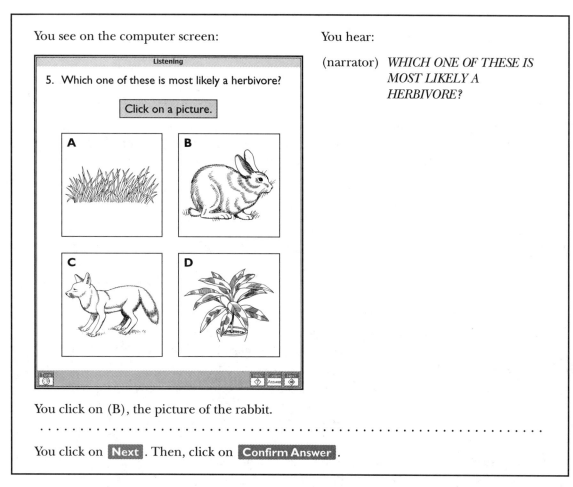

In the lecture, the professor states that *a plant-eating animal is called a herbivore*. From this, it can be inferred that the most likely herbivore in the four pictures is the rabbit. You should click on the drawing of the rabbit in picture B. You need to click on Next and then click on Confirm Answer to proceed to the next question.

After you have clicked on Confirm Answer , another question and answer choices appear on the computer screen as the narrator states the question. This question asks you to click on one of four letters in a diagram to identify the producer.

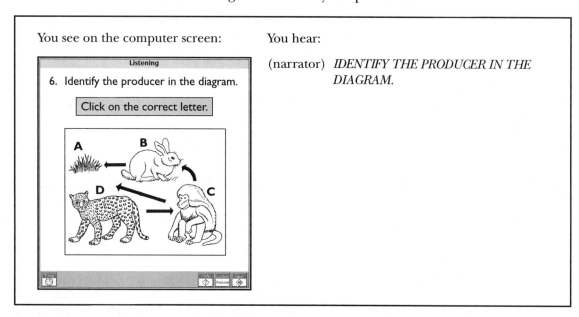

> You click on (A), the grass.
>
> . . . .
>
> You click on **Next** . Then, click on **Confirm Answer** .

In the lecture, the professor states that *a producer is always a plant.* From this you should click on letter A because letter A is the only plant. You need to click on **Next** and then click on **Confirm Answer** to proceed to the next passage.

STRATEGIES FOR THE ACADEMIC LECTURES

1. **Listen carefully to the academic lecture.** You may listen to the lecture one time only.

2. **Use the first visual to help you focus on the context.** The first visual appears on the screen at the beginning of each academic lecture. It shows you that a professor is giving a lecture in an academic lecture hall.

3. **Focus on the overall meaning of the academic lecture rather than on specific words or expressions.** The questions following an academic lecture generally test your overall comprehension of the lecture rather than the meaning of a specific word or expression.

4. **Relate the remaining visuals to the academic lecture.** The remaining visuals are related to the portion of the lecture that you hear as you see the visual.

5. **Listen carefully to each question following the academic lecture as you read it on the screen.** Each listening question is both spoken and written on the computer screen.

6. **Understand the ordering of questions that accompany an academic lecture.** The answers to the questions that accompany a lecture are generally found in order in the lecture. The answer to the first question will generally be found closer to the beginning of the lecture, and the answer to the last question will generally be found closer to the end of the lecture.

7. **Do not panic if you do not understand all of the details of the academic lecture.** You can still answer the questions correctly without understanding each detail of the lecture.

8. **Click on an answer on the computer screen when you have selected an answer.** You may still change your mind at this point and click on a different answer.

9. **Click on Next and then click on Confirm Answer to record your answer.** After you click on this button, you cannot go back and change your answer.

10. **Be prepared for the next question.** After you click on Confirm Answer , the next question begins automatically.

Exercise: **ACADEMIC LECTURES**

DIRECTIONS: Look at the pictures as you listen to each academic lecture. Move from picture to picture when you hear a beep on the tape. Do not look at the questions or answer choices until the lecture is complete. (On the TOEFL® Computer-Based Test, you will not be able to see the questions or answer choices during the lecture.)

Questions 1-5

Listen to a lecture in an astronomy class. The professor is talking about the moons of Jupiter.

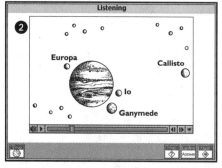

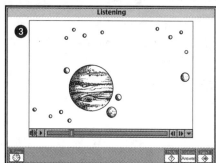

1. How many Galilean satellites are there around Jupiter?
   - ◯ Two
   - ◯ Four
   - ◯ Eight
   - ◯ Sixteen

2. How are these moons characterized?

   Click on a word. Then click on the empty box in the correct column. Use each word only once.

Io	Europa	Ganymede
It is Jupiter's largest moon.	It has volcanic eruptions.	It has a flat and smooth surface.

3. Identify the bodies that scientists believe may be captured asteroids.

   Click on the correct letter.

   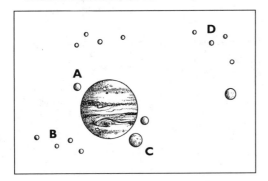

4. Select the moon that most closely resembles Callisto.

   Click on a picture.

   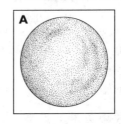 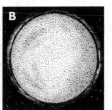

   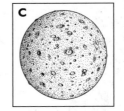 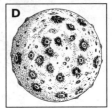

5. What will be the topic of the next lecture?
   - ◯ A different planet
   - ◯ The rings around Jupiter
   - ◯ Other Galilean discoveries
   - ◯ The smallest of Jupiter's satellites

Questions 6-10

Listen to a lecture in a music class. The professor is talking about the trumpet.

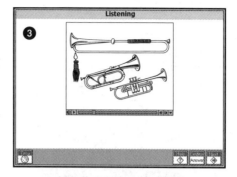

6. What is true about the development of the trumpet?

   Click on 2 answers.

   ☐ It was invented fairly recently.
   ☐ There have been significant changes in its construction.
   ☐ It has been used around the world.
   ☐ Its primary use has traditionally been as a musical instrument.

7. The professor explains the development of the trumpet. Put the types of trumpets in the order in which they were developed.

   Click on a phrase. Then click on the space where it belongs. Use each phrase one time only.

   The addition of valves
   A long, straight tube
   Tubing in a circular loop
   The addition of a bell

1	
2	
3	
4	

8. Which was NOT mentioned as a material from which trumpets have been made?
   ◯ Tusks
   ◯ Stone
   ◯ Cane
   ◯ Silver

9. Identify the trumpet with the most accurate tones.

   Click on a picture.

10. How did the lecturer categorize each of these uses of a trumpet?

    Click on a word. Then click on the empty box in the correct column. Use each word only once.

ceremony	battle	communication
Playing from a mountaintop	Beginning a charge	Announcing an arrival

Questions 11-15

Listen to a lecture in a geography class. The professor is talking about the formation of mountains.

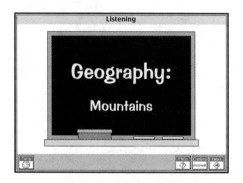

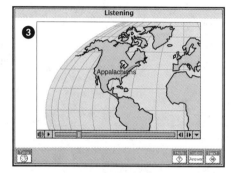

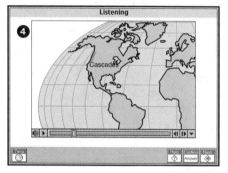

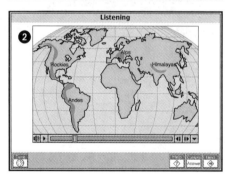

11. The professor explains the order in which mountain ranges developed. Put the ranges in the order in which they developed.

> Click on the name of a mountain range. Then click on the space where it belongs. Use each name one time only.

Andes
Appalachians
Cascades
Rockies

1 [   ]

2 [   ]

3 [   ]

4 [   ]

12. Which of the following mountain ranges are part of the Ring of Fire?

> Click on 2 answers.

☐ The Cascades
☐ The Appalachians
☐ The Rockies
☐ The Andes

13. How long are each of the mountain ranges?

> Click on the name of a mountain range. Then click on the empty box in the correct column. Use each name only once.

Alps	Andes	Rockies
A 3,300-mile range	A 4,500-mile range	Part of a 7,000-mile range

14. Identify the mountain range that is predominantly volcanic in origin.

> Click on the correct letter.

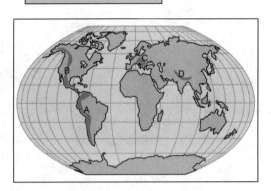

15. What is true about the Appalachians, according to the lecturer?

> Click on 2 answers.

☐ They used to be much taller.
☐ They are volcanic in origin.
☐ They began forming 100 million years ago.
☐ They formed during the collision of plates.

Check your answers in the Answer Key on page 164.
Then turn to page 175 and circle the numbers of the questions that you missed.

TOEFL® COMPUTER-BASED TEST: THE LISTENING SECTION

The following test shows you what the Listening section of the TOEFL® Computer-Based Test looks like. The section begins with a number of Short Dialogues. The remaining questions are a mixture of Casual Conversations, Academic Discussions, and Academic Lectures. During the actual TOEFL® Computer-Based Test, you may take as long as you like to answer each question. You should complete this test in 40 minutes.

DIRECTIONS: Look at the pictures as you hear each listening passage. Do not look at the questions or answer choices until the passage is complete. (On the TOEFL® Computer-Based Test, you will not be able to see the questions or answer choices during the passage.)

1. What can be inferred about the man?
    ◯ He will be far from the conference tonight.
    ◯ He is not quite sure who the speaker will be.
    ◯ He knows Dr. Burton well.
    ◯ He knows that Dr. Burton will be speaking.

2. What does the woman mean?
    ◯ The plane is taking off early.
    ◯ The man needs to make plans soon.
    ◯ The plane is taking up space.
    ◯ The flight is departing in the near future.

3. What does the woman say about the course?
    ◯ The course is free.
    ◯ The course cost $100 more this semester.
    ◯ The course was cheaper last semester.
    ◯ She thinks the cost of the course is too low.

4. What does the woman mean?
   - ◯ The rider took the road to the hospital.
   - ◯ An ambulance took the rider to the hospital.
   - ◯ The ambulance left the hospital with the rider.
   - ◯ The motorcyclist followed the ambulance to the hospital.

5. What does the man mean?
   - ◯ The project that the woman wants is impossible.
   - ◯ Two hours is not long enough to complete the project.
   - ◯ The woman's request can be accomplished.
   - ◯ The woman should not ask for such a thing.

6. What does the man mean?
   - ◯ It was not cold enough.
   - ◯ The snowball struck him forcefully.
   - ◯ The snow stayed around too long.
   - ◯ It was too cold.

7. What does the man say about the art gallery?
   - ◯ He is not very impressed with it.
   - ◯ He thinks it is fantastic.
   - ◯ He does not want more pressure on it.
   - ◯ It is less impressive than expected.

8. What does the woman imply?
   - ◯ She took the stairs out of necessity.
   - ◯ She didn't want to take the elevator.
   - ◯ It was only a few flights of stairs.
   - ◯ She preferred to climb the stairs.

9. What had the man assumed about the woman?
   ◯ That she couldn't get into the lab
   ◯ That she wouldn't do the assignment
   ◯ That her lab assignment was already done
   ◯ That she would start working in a couple of hours

Questions 10-11

10. Why are the students in a hurry?
    ◯ They need to get to sociology class.
    ◯ The library will close soon.
    ◯ They have an hour to finish their reading.
    ◯ The bookstore is not open much longer.

11. Which books must the students have for the sociology course?
    ◯ The text, the workbook, and the study guide
    ◯ The text and the workbook
    ◯ The text and the study guide
    ◯ The workbook and the study guide

Questions 12-13

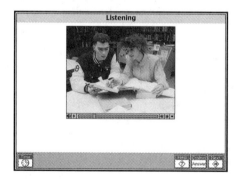

12. On what day does this conversation probably take place?
    ◯ Tuesday
    ◯ Wednesday
    ◯ Thursday
    ◯ Friday

13. What is true about the paper?
    ◯ It should be thirty-five pages long.
    ◯ It can be five double-sided pages.
    ◯ It may not be handwritten.
    ◯ It is due in three days.

Questions 14-17

Listen to a lecture in a history class. The professor is talking about the state of Franklin.

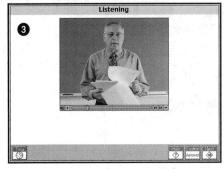

14. When was Franklin a state?
    - ◯ Before North Carolina became a state
    - ◯ For a four-year period in the 17th century
    - ◯ For fourteen years in the 1700s
    - ◯ For a short time in the 18th century

15. What caused the citizens of Franklin to declare statehood?
    - ◯ They were unhappy as citizens of North Carolina.
    - ◯ They no longer had a state government.
    - ◯ The federal government asked them to apply for statehood.
    - ◯ Benjamin Franklin wanted to become a state governor.

16. What happened in the period of time just after Franklin declared itself a state?

    Click on 2 answers.

    - ☐ The federal government took control of the area.
    - ☐ Franklin went to war against North Carolina.
    - ☐ Control was asserted by two different state governments.
    - ☐ The situation in Franklin was unstable.

17. The professor describes a series of historical events. Put the events in order.

    Click on a sentence. Then click on the space where it belongs. Use each sentence one time only.

    Franklin united with North Carolina.

    The Revolutionary War ended.

    Franklin declared itself a state.

    George Washington was elected president.

1	
2	
3	
4	

. . . .

Questions 18-19

18. What is the man's problem?
    - ◯ He always starts studying too early.
    - ◯ He never gets around to studying for exams.
    - ◯ He puts off all his studies until the last moment.
    - ◯ He always does what he intends to do.

19. What does the woman suggest to the man?
    - ◯ Becoming a procrastinator
    - ◯ Making a plan and staying with it
    - ◯ Sticking his neck out on issues
    - ◯ Saying what he intends to accomplish

Questions 20-25

Listen to a discussion by a group of students taking an anatomy class. They are discussing the bones of the human body.

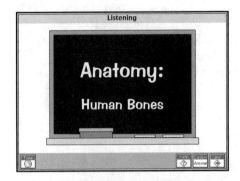

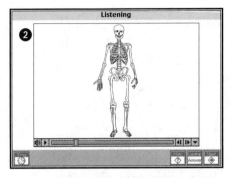

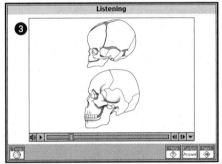

20. How often are quizzes given in the anatomy class that these students are taking?

   ◯ Only on rare occasions
   ◯ Every single day
   ◯ Not at all
   ◯ Almost every class

21. How many bones are there in the human body?

   Click on 2 answers.

   ☐ Two hundred and six in an adult body
   ☐ More than two hundred and six in a baby's body
   ☐ Three hundred in an adult body
   ☐ More than three hundred in a baby's body

22. What happens to some of a baby's bones as the baby grows?

   ◯ They disappear.
   ◯ They defuse.
   ◯ They grow together.
   ◯ They increase in number.

23. What happens to a baby by the age of a year and a half?

   ◯ Its bones have gotten softer.
   ◯ Bone covers the top of its skull.
   ◯ Its skull has separated into two pieces.
   ◯ It has developed a soft spot.

24. Identify the final bone in the body to fuse.

   Click on the correct letter.

25. By what age is bone growth in humans complete?

   ◯ By the age of fifteen
   ◯ No earlier than twenty-five
   ◯ Around the age of fifty
   ◯ No sooner than fifteen

Questions 26-30

Listen to a lecture in a business class. The professor is talking about the early days of the IBM Corporation.

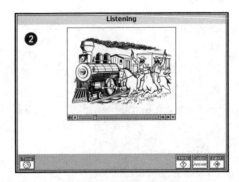

26. What companies have already been discussed in the course?

    | Click on 2 answers. |

    ☐ IBM
    ☐ Coca-Cola®
    ☐ Disney
    ☐ Ford

29. How was the machine that Hollerith developed used?

    ◯ It was used to stop bank robberies.
    ◯ It was used to read cards with census information.
    ◯ It was used to print train tickets.
    ◯ It was used to teach citizens to read.

27. The professor describes a series of events. Put the events in order.

    | Click on a sentence. Then click on the space where it belongs. Use each sentence one time only. |

    Waiting robbers boarded the train.
    Ticketed passengers on board stopped the train.
    The train went to an isolated area.
    The robbers all escaped on horseback.

    1 |_____|
    2 |_____|
    3 |_____|
    4 |_____|

30. In what year did each of these events occur?

    | Click on a date. Then click on the empty box in the correct column. Use each date only once. |

1890	1896	1924
IBM was founded.	The Tabulating Machine Company was started.	A census was run by Hollerith.

28. What proposed solution to the problem of train robbers did the lecturer discuss?

    ◯ Placing additional law officers on trains
    ◯ Having trains not operate on set schedules
    ◯ Recording physical characteristics of passengers on tickets
    ◯ Not selling tickets to train robbers

Check your answers in the Answer Key on page 164.
Then turn to page 175 and circle the numbers of the questions that you missed.

THE STRUCTURE SECTION

The second section of the TOEFL® Computer-Based Test is the Structure section. There are two types of questions in this section of the TOEFL® Computer-Based Test:

1. **Structure** questions consist of sentences in which part has been replaced with a blank. Each sentence is followed by four answer choices. You must choose the answer that completes the sentence in a grammatically correct way.
2. **Written Expression** questions consist of sentences in which four words or groups of words have been underlined. You must choose the underlined word or group of words that is **not** correct.

These two types of questions are intermixed in this section of the test.

The Structure section of the TOEFL® Computer-Based Test is *computer adaptive*. This means that the difficulty of the questions that you see is determined by how well you answer the questions. The section begins with a medium-level question, and the questions that follow will get easier or harder depending on whether or not you answer the questions correctly.

GENERAL STRATEGIES

1. **Be familiar with the directions.** The directions on every TOEFL® Computer-Based Test are the same, so it is not necessary to spend time reading the directions carefully when you take the test. You should be completely familiar with the directions before the day of the test.

2. **Be familiar with computer adaptivity.** This section of the TOEFL® Computer-Based Test is adaptive. This means that you will start with a medium-level question, and the difficulty of the questions will increase or decrease depending on whether or not your answers are correct.

3. **Dismiss the directions as soon as they come up.** The timer starts when the directions come up. You should already be familiar with the directions, so you can click on `Dismiss Directions` as soon as it appears and save all your time for the questions.

4. **Think carefully about a question before you answer it.** You may not return to a question later in the test. You only have one opportunity to answer a given question.

5. **Do not spend too much time on a question you are unsure of.** If you truly do not know the answer to a question, simply guess and go on. The computer will automatically move you into a level of questions that you can answer.

6. **Be very careful not to make careless mistakes.** If you mistakenly choose an incorrect answer, the computer will move you to an easier level of questions than you can handle. You will have to waste time working your way back to the appropriate level of questions.

7. **Monitor the time carefully on the title bar of the computer screen.** The title bar indicates the time remaining in the Structure section, the total number of questions in the section, and the current number.

8. **Do not randomly guess at the end of the section to complete all the questions in the section before time is up.** In a computer adaptive section such as Structure, random guessing to complete the section will only lower your score.

THE STRUCTURE QUESTIONS

The structure questions, which are intermixed with the written expression questions in the Structure section of the TOEFL® Computer-Based Test, test your knowledge of the correct structure of English sentences. The structure questions are multiple choice questions in which you must click on the answer that best completes the sentence.

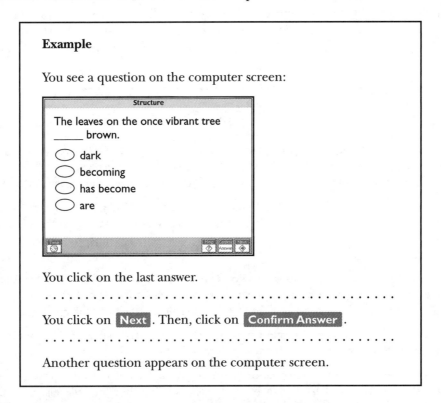

Example

You see a question on the computer screen:

> **Structure**
>
> The leaves on the once vibrant tree _____ brown.
>
> ○ dark
> ○ becoming
> ○ has become
> ○ are

You click on the last answer.

. . . .

You click on Next . Then, click on Confirm Answer .

. . . .

Another question appears on the computer screen.

In this example, you should notice immediately that the sentence has a subject, *leaves*, and that the subject needs a verb. The first and second answers are incorrect because *dark* and *becoming* are not verbs. In the third answer, *has become* is a verb, but *has* is singular and the subject *leaves* is plural. The correct answer is the last answer; *are* is a plural verb. You should therefore click on the last answer on the computer screen. Then, you need to click on Next and click on Confirm Answer to proceed to the next question.

STRATEGIES FOR THE STRUCTURE QUESTIONS

1. **First, study the sentence.** Your purpose is to determine what is needed to complete the sentence correctly.

2. **Then, study each answer based on how well it completes the sentence.** Eliminate answers that do not complete the sentence correctly.

3. **Do not try to eliminate incorrect answers by looking only at the answers.** The incorrect answers are generally correct by themselves. The incorrect answers are generally incorrect only when used to complete the sentence.

4. **Click on an answer on the computer screen when you have selected an answer.** You may still change your mind at this point and click on a different answer.

5. **Click on** Next **and then click on** Confirm Answer **to record your answer.** After you click on the Confirm Answer button, you cannot go back and change your answer. A new question, either a structure question or a written expression question, will appear.

THE WRITTEN EXPRESSION QUESTIONS

The written expression questions, which are intermixed with the structure questions in the Structure section of the TOEFL® Computer-Based Test, test your knowledge of the correct way to express yourself in English writing. Each question in this section consists of one sentence in which four words or groups of words have been underlined. You must click on the underlined word or group of words that is **not** correct.

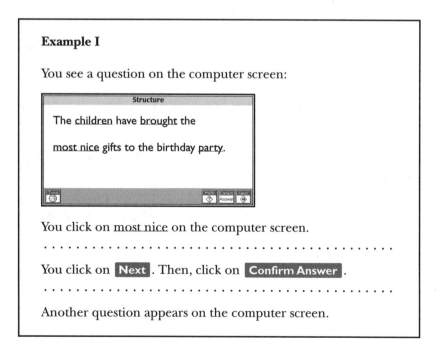

Example I

You see a question on the computer screen:

> **Structure**
>
> The children have brought the
>
> most nice gifts to the birthday party.

You click on most nice on the computer screen.

· ·

You click on Next . Then, click on Confirm Answer .

· ·

Another question appears on the computer screen.

If you look at the underlined words in this example, you should notice immediately that *most nice* is not correct. The correct superlative of *nice* is *nicest*. Therefore, you should click on *most nice* on the computer screen because *most nice* is not correct. Then, you need to click on **Next** and click on **Confirm Answer** to proceed to the next question.

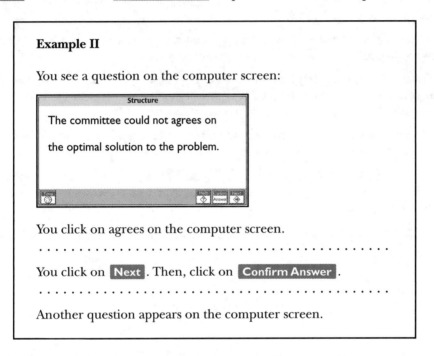

Example II

You see a question on the computer screen:

> **Structure**
>
> The committee could not agrees on
>
> the optimal solution to the problem.

You click on *agrees* on the computer screen.

. . . .

You click on **Next** . Then, click on **Confirm Answer** .

. . . .

Another question appears on the computer screen.

If you look at the underlined words in this example, each word by itself appears to be correct. However, the verb *agrees* is incorrect because it should be in its base form *agree* following the modal *could*. Therefore, you should click on *agrees* on the computer screen because *agrees* is not correct. Then, you need to click on **Next** and click on **Confirm Answer** to proceed to the next question.

STRATEGIES FOR THE WRITTEN EXPRESSION QUESTIONS

1. **First, look at the underlined words or groups of words.** You want to see if you can spot which of the four answer choices is not correct.

2. **If you have been unable to find the error by looking only at the four underlined expressions, then read the complete sentence.** Often an underlined expression is incorrect because of something in another part of the sentence.

3. **Click on one of the underlined answers on the computer screen when you have selected an answer.** You may still change your mind at this point and click on a different answer.

4. **Click on** **Next** **and then click on** **Confirm Answer** **to record your answer.** After you click on the Confirm Answer button, you cannot go back and change your answer. A new question, either a structure question or a written expression question, will appear.

Diagnostic Pre-Test: THE STRUCTURE SECTION

The Diagnostic Pre-Test includes the language skills that will be tested in the Structure section of the TOEFL® Computer-Based Test. You can use the Pre-Test to determine which skills require further work. Then you can practice each of these language skills on the Student CD-ROM. (Each of the language skills tested here is presented comprehensively in *Longman Complete Course for the TOEFL® Test.*)

DIRECTIONS: In questions with underlined words or groups of words, choose the underlined word or group of words that is not correct. In questions with four answer choices, choose the answer that best completes the sentence.

1. The harpsichord is the most complex and most large of all the plucked keyboard instruments.

2. Historical records show that Halley's comet has return about every seventy-six years for the past 2,000 years.

3. Different hormones _____ at the same time on a particular target tissue.
   - ◯ usually act
   - ◯ usually acting
   - ◯ they usually act
   - ◯ the usual action

4. In the cold climate of the far north, mosquito eggs may remains dormant from autumn until late June.

5. The brilliantly colored rhinoceros viper has two or three horns above each nostrils.

6. The tidal forces on the earth due to _____ only 0.46 of those due to the moon.
   - ◯ the sun is
   - ◯ the sun are
   - ◯ the sun it is
   - ◯ the sun they are

7. Alexander Hamilton's advocacy of a strong national government brought he into bitter conflict with Thomas Jefferson.

8. Most of the outer planets has large swarms of satellites surrounding them.

9. Most radioactive elements occur in igneous and metamorphic _____ fossils occur in sedimentary rocks.
   - ◯ rocks, nearly all
   - ◯ rocks, but nearly all
   - ◯ rocks, nearly all are
   - ◯ rocks, which nearly all are

10. Robert Heinlein was instrumental in popularizing science fiction with a series of stories that is first published in the *Saturday Evening Post*.

11. The island of Kauai has <u>much</u> streams, some <u>of which</u> have <u>worn</u> deep canyons into the <u>rock</u>.

12. Each <u>number</u> on the Richter scale <u>represent</u> a tenfold increase in the amplitude of waves of <u>ground motion</u> <u>recorded</u> during an earthquake.

13. _____ radioisotope is encountered, the first step in its identification is the determination of its half-life.
    - ◯ An unknown
    - ◯ Afterwards, an unknown
    - ◯ When an unknown
    - ◯ During an unknown

14. Lake Tahoe, <u>located</u> on the <u>eastern edge</u> of the Sierra Nevada range, is <u>feed</u> by more than thirty mountain <u>streams</u>.

15. Since the dawn of agriculture 9,000 years <u>ago</u>, only a <u>few</u> animal species <u>are</u> domesticated.

16. The Missouri _____ longest river in the United States, flows through seven states from its source in Montana to its confluence with the Mississippi River.
    - ◯ River is the
    - ◯ River, the
    - ◯ River is one of the
    - ◯ River, one of the

17. <u>Established</u> in 1789 and operated by the Jesuits, Georgetown University in Washington D.C. is the <u>older</u> Roman Catholic institution <u>of higher</u> learning <u>in</u> the United States.

18. <u>Most</u> sedimentary rocks <u>start forming</u> when grains of clay, silt, or <u>sandy</u> settle in river valleys <u>or on</u> the bottoms of lakes and oceans.

19. The surface of the planet Venus is <u>almost</u> completely <u>hid</u> by the <u>thick</u> clouds that <u>shroud</u> it.

20. The horn of the rhinoceros consists of a cone of tight bundles of keratin _____ from the epidermis.
    - ◯ grow
    - ◯ grows
    - ◯ growing
    - ◯ they grow

21. <u>Present</u> in rocks of <u>all types</u>, hemetite is <u>particular</u> abundant in the sedimentary rocks <u>known as</u> red beds.

22. Tropical cyclones, <u>alike</u> extratropical cyclones, <u>which</u> derive much <u>of their</u> energy from the jet stream, originate <u>far from</u> the polar front.

23. Elizabeth Cady Stanton organized the first U.S. <u>women's rights convention</u> in 1848 and was <u>instrumentally</u> in the struggle to win <u>voting and property</u> rights for women.

24. Hail forms within large, dense cumulonimbus _____ develop on hot, humid summer days.
    ⬭ clouds
    ⬭ clouds that
    ⬭ clouds that are
    ⬭ clouds that they

25. Jaguarundis are sleek, <u>long-tailed</u> creatures <u>colored</u> either an uniform reddish brown <u>or</u> dark gray.

26. The total thickness of the ventricular <u>walls</u> of the heart <u>are</u> <u>about</u> three times <u>that</u> of the atria.

27. It is possible <u>to get</u> a sunburn on a <u>cloudy</u> day because eighty percent of the ultraviolet rays from the sun <u>would</u> penetrate cloud <u>cover</u>.

28. Measles is a highly contagious viral disease _____ by a characteristic skin rash.
    ⬭ accompany
    ⬭ accompanied
    ⬭ is accompanied
    ⬭ it is accompanied

29. In 1964, GATT established the International Trade Center in order <u>to assist</u> <u>developing</u> countries in the <u>promotion</u> of <u>its</u> exports.

30. Joseph Heller's novel *Catch-22* <u>satirizes</u> both the <u>horrors</u> of war <u>as well as</u> the power of modern <u>bureaucratic</u> institutions.

31. In *Roots*, Alex Haley uses <u>fictional</u> details to <u>embellish</u> a factual <u>histories</u> of seven generations of <u>his</u> family.

32. Charles Darwin's first scientific book, published in 1842, _____ a since substantiated theory on the origin of coral reefs and atolls.
    ⬭ to present
    ⬭ presented
    ⬭ presenting
    ⬭ it presents

33. The <u>carbon atoms</u> of the diamond are <u>so strongly</u> bonded that a diamond can only be <u>scratched</u> with <u>other</u> diamond.

34. <u>Finished</u> in 1936, Boulder Dam <u>has been</u> renamed Hoover Dam in 1947 <u>after</u> ex-President Herbert Hoover.

35. <u>Viruses</u> are <u>extremely</u> tiny parasites that are <u>only able</u> to reproduce within the cells of <u>theirs</u> hosts.

36. Phytoplankters thrive where _____ phosphorus into the upper layers of a body of water.
    ⬭ upwelling currents circulate
    ⬭ the circulation of upwelling currents
    ⬭ are upwelling currents
    ⬭ circulates upwelling currents

37. William Henry Harrison, a ninth president of the United States, <u>died</u> of pneumonia after <u>serving</u> only one month <u>in office</u>.

38. During the last Ice Age, <u>which</u> ended about 10,000 years ago, there was about three times <u>more</u> ice than <u>is</u> today.

39. By the end of 1609, Galileo had a 20-power telescope that enabled him to see _____ planets revolving around Jupiter.
    - ◯ the call
    - ◯ he called
    - ◯ to call him
    - ◯ what he called

40. <u>Surrounded</u> by forested mountain <u>slopes are</u> the town of Telluride, a <u>former</u> gold-mining town 7,500 feet above <u>sea level</u>.

41. Coral islands such as the Maldives are the tips of reefs built during periods of warm climate, when _____ higher.
    - ◯ were sea levels
    - ◯ sea had levels
    - ◯ having sea levels
    - ◯ sea levels were

42. Melons <u>most probably</u> originated in Persia and were <u>introduced</u> the North American continent <u>during</u> the sixteenth century.

43. Many bugs possess defensive scent glands and emit disagreeable odors when _____.
    - ◯ disturbed
    - ◯ are disturbed
    - ◯ they disturbed
    - ◯ are they disturbed

44. Hurricanes move with the large-scale wind currents _____ are imbedded.
    - ◯ that they
    - ◯ which they
    - ◯ in that they
    - ◯ in which they

45. Humans <u>develop normally</u> twenty <u>primary</u>, <u>or</u> deciduous, teeth and thirty-two <u>permanent</u> teeth.

46. More than 600 <u>million</u> individual <u>bacteria</u> <u>lives</u> on the skin of <u>humans</u>.

47. The extinct Martian volcano Olympus Mons is approximately three times as _____ Mount Everest.
    - ◯ high
    - ◯ high as is
    - ◯ higher than
    - ◯ the highest of

48. The <u>city</u> of Houston <u>named after</u> Sam Houston, <u>the first</u> president of the Republic of Texas.

49. Indonesia's Komodo dragon is the largest <u>alive</u> lizard, <u>attaining</u> a total <u>length of up to</u> three meters.

50. The more directly overhead the moon is, _____ that it exhibits on the earth.
    - ◯ the effect is greater
    - ◯ the great effect is
    - ◯ its great effect
    - ◯ the greater is the effect

51. Mauna Kea's upper slopes have caves <u>where</u> ancient Hawaiians <u>dug</u> basalt and <u>used it</u> to <u>do</u> tools.

52. <u>Shortly</u> before the Allied <u>invader</u> of Normandy, Ernest Hemingway moved to London <u>as a</u> war <u>correspondent</u> for *Collier's*.

53. Only when air and water seep through its outer coat _____.
    - ◯ to the germination of a seed
    - ◯ a seed germinates
    - ◯ for a seed to germinate
    - ◯ does a seed germinate

54. Spenser Tracy <u>won</u> Academy Awards for <u>his</u> performances as <u>fisherman</u> in *Captains Courageous* (1937) <u>and</u> as Father Flanagan in *Boys Town* (1938).

55. <u>As the</u> International Dateline at 180 degrees longitude is crossed <u>westerly</u>, it becomes <u>necessary</u> to change the date <u>by moving</u> it one day forward.

56. On every continent except Antartica _____ more than 30,000 species of spiders.
    - ◯ some are
    - ◯ some of the
    - ◯ is some
    - ◯ are some of the

57. Kilauea's <u>numerous</u> eruptions are generally comprised <u>in</u> molten lava, with <u>little</u> escaping gas and <u>few</u> explosions.

58. _____ seasonal rainfall, especially in regions near the tropics, is winds that blow in an opposite direction in winter than in summer.
    - ◯ Causing
    - ◯ That cause
    - ◯ What causes
    - ◯ To cause

59. The <u>incubation</u> period of tetanus is usually five to ten days, and <u>the most</u> frequently <u>occurred</u> symptom is jaw <u>stiffness</u>.

60. _____ the earth's ice to melt, the earth's oceans would rise by about two hundred feet.
    - ◯ If all
    - ◯ Were all
    - ◯ If all were
    - ◯ All was

Check your answers in the Answer Key on page 165.
Then turn to page 176 and circle the numbers of the questions that you missed.

Post-Test: THE STRUCTURE SECTION

> The Post-Test includes the language skills that will be tested in the Structure section of the TOEFL® Computer-Based Test. You can use the Post-Test to measure your proficiency after you have completed the related sections on the Student CD-ROM.

DIRECTIONS: In questions with underlined words or groups of words, choose the underlined word or group of words that is not correct. In questions with four answer choices, choose the answer that best completes the sentence.

1. The wave <u>lengths</u> of ultraviolet light are <u>short</u> than <u>those</u> of visible light <u>but</u> longer than those of X-rays.

2. All thoroughbreds are descended <u>from</u> three Oriental <u>stallion</u> imported <u>into</u> England between 1689 and 1724.

3. The planet Mercury _____ rotations during every two trips around the Sun.
   - ○ three complete
   - ○ completes three
   - ○ the completion of three
   - ○ completing three of the

4. By <u>measuring</u> the rate of decay of potassium isotopes in volcanic ash, scientists <u>can date</u> the layers of volcanic ash <u>and any</u> human remains in <u>they</u>.

5. Most polar seals <u>retreat</u> to open water during the winter, but <u>a few</u> types have <u>learn</u> to survive on and under the ice all year <u>round</u>.

6. In prehistoric _____ of western Utah was covered by Lake Bonneville.
   - ○ times, a large part
   - ○ times, there was a large part
   - ○ part of the time
   - ○ for large parts of time

7. <u>Hundreds of</u> partial <u>to complete</u> fossil skeletons of *Triceratops* have been <u>gather</u> in North America from <u>rocks</u> of the late Cretaceous period.

8. <u>More than</u> half <u>of all</u> stars <u>is</u> in binary <u>or</u> multiple-star systems.

9. The helicopter is able to hover in _____ powered rotors produce lift even at zero forward speed.
   - ○ flight because the
   - ○ flying the
   - ○ the flying of the
   - ○ flight because of the

10. <u>United States forces</u> won the city of Los Angeles in 1847 <u>during</u> the Mexican War and <u>gain</u> all of California in the same year.

11. High blood pressure <u>results from</u> either an <u>increased</u> output of blood from the heart <u>and</u> an increased resistance to its <u>flow</u> through tiny branches of the arteries.

12. The upper levels of the sun's atmosphere are of very low _____ heats the gases there to very high temperatures.
    ○ dense and solar
    ○ density, solar activity
    ○ density, but solar activity
    ○ density and activity of the sun is

13. Thirty-one <u>pairs</u> of spinal nerves <u>are present</u> in humans, and each pair <u>have</u> two roots.

14. W. Somerset Maugham's <u>best-known</u> novel, *Of Human Bondage*, is <u>a partially</u> fictionalized account <u>of a</u> unhappy <u>youth</u>.

15. By the <u>time of</u> the dinosaurs, turtles <u>have</u> already developed the hard shell <u>into which</u> their heads and legs could be <u>drawn</u>.

16. Lapis lazuli, _____ stone, has been valued for ornamental purposes for more than 6,000 years.
    ○ an opaque deep blue
    ○ is an opaque deep blue
    ○ it is an opaque deep blue
    ○ that is an opaque deep blue

17. <u>The big</u> island of Hawaii is more <u>volcanically active</u> than the <u>others</u> islands in the archipelago.

18. <u>Probably the best known</u> of all dinosaurs, the *Tyrannosaurus* was <u>larger</u> and <u>last</u> of the meat-eating carnosaurs.

19. The leaves and young twigs of the henna plant are <u>ground</u> into a powder to <u>produce</u> a <u>paste that</u> can <u>used</u> as a dye.

20. Mountaineers _____ climb Mount Everest must make reservations to do so, often up to seven years in advance.
    ○ want to
    ○ they want to
    ○ wanting to
    ○ who want

21. The Washington <u>quarter</u> was <u>first minting</u> by the U.S. government in 1932 on the 200th <u>anniversary</u> of George Washington's birth.

22. The Congressional Medal of Honor, instituted at the <u>height</u> of the Civil War, is today a highest <u>decoration</u> for <u>gallantry</u> in the United States.

23. Created by the dissolution of limestone, the underground cave system _____ Mammoth Cave is noted for its stalactites and stalagmites.
    ○ is known as
    ○ it is known to be
    ○ known as
    ○ to be known

24. Hardwood <u>comes from</u> broad-leaved <u>deciduous</u> trees, <u>those that</u> lose <u>theirs</u> leaves in winter.

25. James A. Garfield <u>has become</u> the <u>twentieth</u> president of the United States in 1881 and <u>was assassinated</u> later <u>in that</u> year.

26. Most slang terms are simply old words _____ additional new meanings.
    ◯ give
    ◯ given
    ◯ are given
    ◯ they are given

27. William Randolph Hearst <u>built</u> a chain of newspapers <u>that</u> included 25 <u>dailies</u> and 11 Sunday editions at <u>their</u> peak in 1937.

28. The Kentucky Derby is <u>held in</u> the first Saturday <u>in May</u> at the Churchill Downs <u>racetrack in</u> Louisville, Kentucky.

29. _____ manipulate with their feet as well as with their hands, it is difficult for them to stand upright.
    ◯ Apes can, however,
    ◯ Apes are able to
    ◯ Although apes can
    ◯ Despite the ability of apes

30. Manganese, <u>found</u> in trace amounts in higher animals, activates a large <u>amount</u> of the enzymes <u>involved</u> in metabolic <u>processes</u>.

31. Lemon trees are similar <u>in</u> longevity and <u>appear</u> to orange trees <u>but have</u> more upright <u>growth</u>.

32. North Carolina's Outer Banks are a chain of low, narrow islands _____ the mainland from the frequent Atlantic storms in the area.
    ◯ they buffer
    ◯ that buffer
    ◯ to buffer them
    ◯ that they buffer

33. Mambas, <u>poisonous</u> African snakes that <u>come from</u> the same family as cobras, possess an <u>extreme</u> potent venom.

34. Christopher Columbus, <u>alike</u> <u>many</u> <u>other</u> explorers, underestimated the size of the earth and overestimated the <u>width</u> of Asia.

35. The film *Lawrence of Arabia* is three hours and forty-one minutes long, one minute _____ *Gone With the Wind*.
    ◯ longer than is
    ◯ long is
    ◯ is longer than
    ◯ in length like

36. The remains of *Homo erectus*, an extinct <u>species</u> of early man, <u>was</u> first <u>discovered</u> on the island of Java by Dutch physician Eugene Dubois.

37. The Ford Motor Company introduced the <u>moving</u> assembly line in 1914 so that it <u>will</u> be able to meet the huge <u>demand</u> for <u>its</u> Model T.

38. The genus *Equus* became extinct in North America during the glacial period, and it was not reintroduced until _____ by the Spaniards.
   ◯ brought there
   ◯ was brought there
   ◯ bringing it there
   ◯ it brought there

39. By 1830, approximately 200 steamboats had become operationally on the Mississippi River.

40. Not until the discovery of Pluto's moon Charon was many of the characteristics of the planet Pluto evident.

41. It is at the age of approximately eighteen months _____ children begin to make combinations of two or three words.
   ◯ when do many
   ◯ when are many
   ◯ when many
   ◯ when have many of the

42. Scorpions, which are normally lone, have developed a cautious mating ritual because they are not immune to their own poison.

43. The huge Meteor Crater was created when a 63,000 ton iron meteorites struck the earth near Winslow, Arizona.

44. *Story of a Bad Boy,* a semiautobiographical novel by Thomas Bailey Aldrich, ranks high among books _____ have incorporated their boyhood experiences.
   ◯ that American authors
   ◯ which are American authors
   ◯ in which American authors
   ◯ are those which American authors

45. The Appalachian Mountains extend Georgia and Alabama in the south to Canada in the north.

46. Howard Hughes once did more than half a billion dollars in one day in 1966 when he received a single bank draft for $546,549,171 for his share of TWA.

47. In the La Brea tar pits of Los Angeles _____ which have been preserved from the Pleistocene period.
   ◯ thousands of animals are
   ◯ thousands are animals
   ◯ the thousands of animals
   ◯ are thousands of animals

48. The diameter of the sun is more than one hundred times greater than the earth.

49. The shapes of snow crystals depend largely _____ temperature and humidity are.
   ◯ how high its
   ◯ on the height of the
   ◯ on how high the
   ◯ that the height of the

50. The city of Tampa, Florida, is <u>located</u> on <u>peninsula</u> across Tampa Bay <u>from</u> Saint Petersburg.

51. _____ to December 21, the first day of winter, the shorter the days become.
    - ○ It gets closer
    - ○ To get it closer
    - ○ The closer it gets
    - ○ Getting it closer

52. Daniel Boone <u>helped to</u> build the Wilderness Road <u>through</u> the Cumberland Gap, <u>creating</u> a route for settlers heading <u>westerly</u>.

53. <u>Only about</u> a hundred out of an <u>estimating</u> 3,000 known mineral <u>species</u> have been found at least reasonably suitable <u>for use</u> as gems.

54. _____ provided a living for nearly 90 percent of the population of the American colonies.
    - ○ Farming was what
    - ○ What farming
    - ○ Farming was
    - ○ What was farming

55. Paul Revere was the son of a French <u>immigration</u> named Apollos Rivoire, <u>who</u> later began calling <u>himself</u> Revere to make his name <u>easier</u> for Americans to pronounce.

56. Most <u>of the</u> year, San Miguel Island is <u>shrouded</u> in fog, and <u>strong</u> northwest winds batter <u>relentlessly the island</u>.

57. Not only _____ more brittle than hard maples, but they are also less able to withstand high winds.
    - ○ soft maples are
    - ○ are soft maples
    - ○ they are soft maples
    - ○ soft maples

58. Women have <u>admitted</u> to the United States Military Academy at West Point <u>since</u> 1976, and the <u>first</u> women cadets <u>graduated</u> in 1980.

59. Related <u>fungus</u> from a family of yeasts <u>called</u> ascomycetes cause <u>bread</u> to rise, create the veins in blue cheese, and <u>produce</u> penicillin.

60. _____ become blocked so that heat and moisture could not escape, death would result.
    - ○ Were the skin's pores to
    - ○ The pores of the skin were to
    - ○ The skin's pores
    - ○ If the pores of the skin

Check your answers in the Answer Key on pages 165-166.
Then turn to page 176 and circle the numbers of the questions that you missed.

TOEFL® Computer-Based Test: THE STRUCTURE SECTION

The following test shows you what the Structure section of the TOEFL® Computer-Based Test looks like. On the CBT, you may be asked to complete twenty questions in fifteen minutes (or you may have a longer version of the test), and the structure questions and the written expression questions are mixed together. On the actual CBT, the Structure section is *adaptive* (the questions get easier or harder depending on whether you answer correctly or incorrectly), but it is not possible to make a test in a book adaptive.

DIRECTIONS: In questions with underlined words or groups of words, choose the underlined word or group of words that is not correct. In questions with four answer choices, choose the answer that best completes the sentence.

1. The price of silver rose to $50.05 per troy ounce in January 1980 and then fell to $10.80 two month later.

2. The language with the largest alphabet is Cambodian, with 74 letters, while the most short is the Solomon Island language of Rotokas, with only 11.

3. In the late 1880s, Hull House _____ United States' first welfare center.
   - ◯ to become
   - ◯ became the
   - ◯ becoming one of the
   - ◯ it became

4. During fermentation, complex carbohydrates are converted to another chemicals by the action of enzymes produced by molds, yeasts, or bacteria.

5. _____ given to the various types of microscopic plants and animals found in water.
   - ◯ Named plankton
   - ◯ The name of plankton
   - ◯ Plankton's name
   - ◯ Plankton is the name

6. The surface of Mars is very complex and consists of a mixture of flat deserts, craters, volcanoes, and mountainous.

7. Charles Babbage (1792–1871) drew up the first plans for a programmable digital computer in 1834, but _____ was never completed.
   - ◯ his invention
   - ◯ he invented
   - ◯ to invent him
   - ◯ for him to invent

8. In a honeybee hive is several vertically aligned honeycombs with hexagonal wax cells stacked close together.

9. Approximately 500 varieties of insectivorous plants, which trap animals for their sustenance, _____ in the world.
   - ⭕ and their existence
   - ⭕ exist
   - ⭕ they exist
   - ⭕ that exist

10. As a <u>protection device</u>, an octopus ejects black <u>or</u> purple ink <u>to cloud</u> the water while it <u>escaped</u>.

11. When the U.S. <u>government's</u> library was <u>burned by</u> the British in 1814, <u>former</u> President Thomas Jefferson donated 6,487 of <u>their</u> own books to start the present-day Library of Congress.

12. In the <u>mid-18th</u> century, American, Russian, and Canadian hunters <u>on the</u> Pacific coast of North America <u>annihilated almost</u> the sea otter in order <u>to collect</u> the pelts.

13. Ozone is formed when ultraviolet radiation from the sun _____ molecules into highly reactive oxygen atoms.
    - ⭕ oxygen breaks up
    - ⭕ oxygen is broken up
    - ⭕ breaks up oxygen
    - ⭕ to break up oxygen

14. Pat Garrett, who <u>shot and killed</u> Billy the Kid on July 14, 1881, <u>later</u> did his living <u>as a</u> Texas Ranger.

15. <u>Safety glass</u>, a <u>toughened</u> glass sheet, is six <u>times stronger</u> than <u>untreating</u> glass.

16. The surrealistic movement in art in the 1920s and 1930s placed _____ is pictured in the unconscious and often incorporated dreamlike images.
    - ⭕ to emphasize it
    - ⭕ an emphasis on it
    - ⭕ emphasize what
    - ⭕ an emphasis on what

17. The foxglove is <u>source</u> of the drug digitalis, <u>which is</u> <u>used to</u> treat <u>heart disease</u>.

18. Today used to measure the weight of gemstones or the amount of gold per 24 parts of pure gold, _____ originally the weight of a seed of the carob tree.
    - ⭕ was a carat
    - ⭕ a carat was
    - ⭕ which was a carat
    - ⭕ that a carat was

19. Cuneiform <u>writing, one</u> of the oldest <u>forms</u> of written communication, <u>used</u> <u>as early as</u> 3000 B.C.

20. <u>Rival</u> leaders <u>during</u> the American Civil War, Abraham Lincoln and Jefferson Davis <u>both</u> <u>hailed</u> Kentucky.

Check your answers in the Answer Key on page 166.
Then turn to page 176 and circle the numbers of the questions that you missed.

THE READING SECTION

The third section of the TOEFL® Computer-Based Test is the Reading section. In this part of the test you will be given a number of reading passages, each followed by a series of reading comprehension and vocabulary questions. Topics of the reading passages are varied, but they are often informational subjects that might be studied in an American university: American history, literature, art, architecture, geology, geography, and astronomy, for example.

GENERAL STRATEGIES

1. **Be familiar with the directions.** The directions on every TOEFL® Computer-Based Test are the same, so it is not necessary to spend time reading the directions carefully when you take the test. You should be completely familiar with the directions before the day of the test.

2. **Understand that this section of the test is linear rather than computer adaptive.** This means that the ordering of the passages and questions is specified (and is not determined by how the test-taker has answered previous questions). The reading passages progress from easy-to-difficult, and the order of the questions is based on the location of the answers in the passage (just as they were on the paper-and-pencil TOEFL® test).

3. **Dismiss the directions as soon as they come up.** The timer starts when the directions come up. You should already be familiar with the directions, so you can hit [Dismiss Directions] as soon as it appears and save all your time for the questions.

4. **Do not spend too much time on a question you are unsure of.** If you do not know the answer to a question, simply guess and go on. You can return to this question later in the section if you have time.

5. **Monitor the time carefully on the title bar of the computer screen.** The title bar indicates the time remaining in the Reading section, the total number of questions in the section, and the current number.

6. **Guess to complete the section before time is up.** Because this section is linear rather than adaptive, it can only increase your score to guess the answers to questions that you do not have time to complete.

THE READING QUESTIONS

Each reading passage will be accompanied by a mix of three different types of questions.

1. **Multiple Choice** questions ask you to select the best answers to questions about the information given in the reading passages. A multiple choice question may ask about the main ideas, directly answered details, indirectly answered details, vocabulary, or overall review ideas.

2. **Click-on** questions ask you to find a word, phrase, sentence, or paragraph in a passage that answers a question and to click on that word, phrase, sentence, or paragraph. They may also ask you to click on one of four pictures following a passage. In a click-on question, you may be asked to find and click on a vocabulary word with a specific meaning, a reference for a particular pronoun, a sentence or picture that answers a detail question, or a paragraph that develops a main idea.

3. **Insertion** questions ask you to find the most logical place in a passage to insert a specific piece of information. In an insertion question, you may be asked to insert a sentence that expresses a main idea, a supporting detail or example, a transition, or a concluding idea into the appropriate place in a passage.

STRATEGIES FOR THE READING QUESTIONS

1. **Scroll through the reading passage to determine the main idea and the overall organization of ideas in the passage.** You do not need to understand every detail in each passage to answer the questions correctly. It is therefore a waste of time to read the passage with the intent of understanding every single detail before you try to answer the questions. When you have finished scrolling quickly through the passage, click on Proceed to begin the first question.

2. **As the question comes up on the screen, look at the question type to find the section of the passage that deals with that question.** The question type tells you exactly where to look in the passage to find the correct answer.
   - For *main idea questions,* look at the first line of each paragraph.
   - For *directly* and *indirectly answered detail questions,* choose a key word in the question, and skim for that key word (or a related idea) in order in the passage.
   - For *vocabulary questions,* the vocabulary will be highlighted in the passage.
   - For *overall review questions,* the answers are found anywhere in the passage.

4. **Read the part of the passage that contains the answer carefully.** The answer will probably be in the same sentence (or one sentence before or after) the key word or idea.

5. **Choose the best answer to each question.** You can choose the best answer according to what is given in the appropriate section of the passage, or you can eliminate definitely wrong answers and select your best guess on the computer screen.

6. **Click on the answer on the computer screen when you have selected an answer.** You may still change your mind at this point and click on a different answer. You may also return to a question later.

Question Type 1: MULTIPLE CHOICE QUESTIONS

Multiple choice questions are one of the three types of questions that may accompany a reading passage on the TOEFL® Computer-Based Test. Similar to the paper-and-pencil TOEFL®, the TOEFL® Computer-Based Test uses multiple choice questions to test the **main ideas** of reading passages, **directly answered detail** questions, **indirectly answered detail** questions, **vocabulary** questions, or **overall review** questions.

In a multiple choice question, you are asked to choose which of four answer choices best answers a question and select the best answer on the computer screen. For some questions, you may also be asked to choose two correct answers. The following passage is accompanied by examples of the various types of multiple choice questions that you might encounter on the TOEFL® Computer-Based Test.

Example

You see part of the passage and the first question on the computer screen.

· ·

You scroll through the passage to find the answer.

Reading

One of the most important events in the history of life on Earth was the movement of life out of the water and onto land. In all probability, the first living things on land were simple one-celled plants, the first of which left the water more than a billion years ago. It took more than 500 million years for complicated plants to move out of the water and develop ways to survive on land.

Plant life moved onto land before animal life most probably because plant life was able to make use of the raw materials found on land, such as minerals found in the soil and sunlight, to develop mechanisms for survival. Animals, however, needed firmly established and abundant plant life on land to provide food before they were able to move out of the water and adapt to life on land.

It was not until some 400 million years ago that plants were firmly established on land and animals were able to move out of the water. It is likely that the first animals came out of the water in search of food and found plant life on land abundant enough to provide for their needs. These first land animals were probably small plant-eating arthropods, such as the millipede, which feasted on decayed vegetation. These plant-eating arthropods were later followed by predatory meat-eating arthropods, the first of which was the scorpion.

1. Which of the following best states the topic of the passage?

○ The movement of plant life from water to land

○ The history of plants and animals

○ When animals moved out of the water

○ The evolutionary move of life forms from water to land

You click on the last answer.

· ·

> You click on   Next .
>
> . . . .
>
> Another question appears on the computer screen.

This first question asks about the **topic** of the passage, so you should concentrate on the first line of each paragraph to answer the question. The entire passage may not fit on the screen at once, so you may have to scroll through the passage to see the first line of each paragraph. As you read the first line of the first paragraph, you should understand that the first paragraph is probably an introduction to the passage. The first line of this paragraph discusses the *movement of life out of the water and onto land.* The second and third paragraphs are supporting paragraphs that tell you that *plant life moved onto land* and that *animals were able to move out of the water.* This paragraph therefore discusses the movement of both plants and animals out of the water and onto land. The first answer is incorrect because it only mentions plant life and not animal life, and the third answer is incorrect because it only mentions animal life and not plant life. The second answer is too general: it mentions both plants and animals but does not mention what happened with these life forms. The best answer to the question is the last answer, which includes both plants and animals in *life forms* and mentions their *evolutionary move...to land.* You should therefore click on the last answer on the computer screen. Then, click on   Next   to move to the next question.

After you have clicked on   Next , another question appears in the question box on the computer screen. The second question is a **vocabulary** question that asks about replacing the word *mechanisms.* You should scroll to the part of the passage that includes the highlighted word *mechanisms,* carefully read the sentence that contains *mechanisms,* and try each of the answer choices in the sentence in place of *mechanisms.*

> You see part of the passage and the second question on the computer screen.
>
> . . . .
>
> You scroll through the passage to find the answer.
>
> | Reading |
> |---|
>
> Plant life moved onto land before animal life most probably because plant life was able to make use of the raw materials found on land, such as minerals found in the soil and sunlight, to develop mechanisms for survival. Animals, however, needed firmly established and abundant plant life on land to provide food before they were able to move out of the water and adapt to life on land.
>
> 2. The word mechanisms could best be replaced by which of the following?
>
> ◯ Machines
> ◯ Processes
> ◯ Cravings
> ◯ Nutrients
>
> You click on the second answer.
>
> . . . .
>
> You click on   Next .
>
> . . . .
>
> Another question appears on the computer screen.

Since *mechanisms* can be *methods* or *processes* and since this meaning of *mechanisms* fits into the sentence, the best answer to this question is the second answer. You should click on the second answer on the computer screen. Then, click on **Next** to move to the next question.

After you have clicked on **Next**, a new question will appear on the screen. The expression *according to the passage* in the third question indicates that this is a **directly answered detail** question, and this question is about the situation *400 million years ago*. You should scroll through the passage and skim to find the part of the passage that mentions *400 million years ago;* this part of the passage will most probably be after the line in the passage where *mechanisms* is found because the answer to the third question probably follows the answer to the second question. When you find the appropriate part of the passage, read it carefully.

You see part of the passage and the third question on the computer screen.

· ·

You scroll through the passage to find the answer.

Reading

It was not until some 400 million years ago that plants were firmly established on land and animals were able to move out of the water. It is likely that the first animals came out of the water in search of food and found plant life on land abundant enough to provide for their needs.

3. What was the situation 400 million years ago, according to the passage?

○ Animals were already on land.
○ Plants were already on land.
○ Animals were not yet living in water.
○ Plants began moving to land.

You click on the second answer.

· ·

You click on **Next**.

· ·

Another question appears on the computer screen.

The passage states that *400 million years ago...plants were firmly established on land,* so the best answer to this question is the second answer. You should click on the second answer on the computer screen. Then, click on **Next** to move to the next question.

After you have clicked on **Next**, a new question appears on the screen. The word *likely* in the fourth question indicates that this is an **indirectly answered detail** question. Because the answer to this question probably comes after the answer to the third question, you should scroll to the part of the passage following the section that contains the answer to the previous question. The answers to the fourth question mention *millipede* or *scorpion*, so the final part of the passage probably contains clues leading to the best answer to this question.

You see part of the passage and the fourth question on the computer screen.

· ·

You scroll through the passage to find the answer.

Reading	
These first land animals were probably small plant-eating arthropods, such as the millipede, which feasted on decayed vegetation. These plant-eating arthropods were later followed by predatory meat-eating arthropods, the first of which was the scorpion.	4. Which of the following would be more likely? ◯ A millipede would attack and eat a scorpion. ◯ A millipede would attack and eat another millipede. ◯ A scorpion would feast on decayed vegetation. ◯ A scorpion would attack and eat a millipede.

You click on the last answer.

· ·

You click on **Next** .

· ·

Another question appears on the computer screen.

The passage states that a millipede is *plant-eating*, so a millipede would probably not attack and eat either a scorpion (the first answer), or another millipede (the second answer). The passage states that a scorpion is *meat-eating*, so a scorpion would probably not eat decayed vegetation (the third answer) but might possibly eat a millipede (the last answer). The best answer to this question is therefore the last answer, so you should click on the last answer on the computer screen. Then, click on **Next** to move to the next question.

After you have clicked on **Next** , another question appears on the computer screen. The word *courses* in this question indicates that this is an **overall review** question. Since this is an **overall review** question, you should look at the first line of each paragraph to understand the main ideas of the passage.

You see part of the passage and the fifth question on the screen.

· ·

You scroll through the passage to read the beginning of each paragraph.

Reading	
One of the most important events in the history of life on Earth was the movement of life out of the water and onto land . . . . 　　Plant life moved onto land before animal life . . . . 　　It was not until some 400 million years ago that plants were firmly established on land and animals were able to move out of the water	5. This passage might be assigned reading in which of the following courses? ◯ Contemporary History ◯ Evolutionary Biology ◯ Molecular Chemistry ◯ Cultural Anthropology

> You click on the second answer.
>
> . . . .
>
> You click on `Next` .
>
> . . . .
>
> Another question appears on the computer screen.

The first sentence of the first paragraph mentions *the movement of life out of the water and onto land,* and the first sentences of the next two paragraphs state that *plant life moved onto land before animal life* and that *400 million years ago...animals were able to move out of the water.* It can be inferred from this information that this reading might be assigned in a course on *evolutionary biology,* so you should click on the second answer on the computer screen. Then, click on `Next` to move to the next question.

The following chart outlines the key information that you should remember about multiple choice questions on the TOEFL® Computer-Based Test:

THE MULTIPLE CHOICE QUESTION	
WHAT IT TESTS	• a main idea • a directly answered detail • an indirectly answered detail • vocabulary • an overall review idea
HOW IT IS RELATED TO THE PAPER-AND-PENCIL TEST	It is basically the same type of question that is found on the paper-and-pencil test, although there may be two correct answers. It tests many of the same skills that are found on the paper-and-pencil test.
HOW IT IS RELATED TO SKILLS IN *VOLUME A*	Many of the reading and vocabulary skills presented in *Volume A* are covered in the multiple choice questions on the TOEFL® Computer-Based Test: • Skills 1-2 (*Questions about the Ideas of the Passage*) • Skills 3-4 (*Directly Answered Questions*) • Skills 6-7 (*Indirectly Answered Questions*) • Skills 8-11 (*Vocabulary Questions*) • Skill 13 (*Overall Review Questions*)
WHERE ITS ANSWER CAN BE FOUND	For a **main idea** question or an **overall review** question, the answer can generally be determined by looking at the first sentence of each paragraph. For *other* types of questions, the answers are found in order in the passage.
HOW YOU SHOULD ANSWER IT	1. Skim and scroll through the passage to find the appropriate place in the passage. 2. Read that part of the passage carefully. 3. Eliminate the definitely wrong answers, and choose the best answer from the remaining choices. 4. Click on the best answer on the computer screen.

Exercise: MULTIPLE CHOICE QUESTIONS

Study each of the passages, and choose the best answers to the questions that follow. In this exercise, each passage is followed by a number of multiple choice questions of the type that you might find on the TOEFL® Computer-Based Test. (On the actual TOEFL® Computer-Based Test, the multiple choice questions are intermixed with the other types of questions.)

PASSAGE ONE (Questions 1-10)

A rather surprising geographical feature of Antarctica is that a huge freshwater lake, one of the world's largest and deepest, lies hidden there under four kilometers of ice. Now known as Lake Vostok, this huge body of water is located under the ice block that comprises Antarctica. The lake is able to exist in its unfrozen state beneath this block of ice because its waters are warmed by geothermal heat from the earth's core. The thick glacier above Lake Vostok actually insulates it from the frigid temperatures (the lowest ever recorded on earth) on the surface.

The lake was first discovered in the 1970s while a research team was conducting an aerial survey of the area. Radio waves from the survey equipment penetrated the ice and revealed a body of water of indeterminate size. It was not until much more recently that data collected by satellite made scientists aware of the tremendous size of the lake; the satellite-borne radar detected an extremely flat region where the ice remains level because it is floating on the water of the lake.

The discovery of such a huge freshwater lake trapped under Antarctica is of interest to the scientific community because of the potential that the lake contains ancient microbes that have survived for thousands upon thousands of years, unaffected by factors such as nuclear fallout and elevated ultraviolet light that have affected organisms in more exposed areas. The downside of the discovery, however, lies in the difficulty of conducting research on the lake in such a harsh climate and in the problems associated with obtaining uncontaminated samples from the lake without actually exposing the lake to contamination. Scientists are looking for possible ways to accomplish this.

1. The purpose of the passage is to
   - ◯ explain how Lake Vostok was discovered
   - ◯ provide satellite data concerning Antarctica
   - ◯ discuss future plans for Lake Vostok
   - ◯ present an unexpected aspect of Antarctica's geography

2. The word lies in paragraph 1 could best be replaced by
   - ◯ sleeps
   - ◯ sits
   - ◯ tells falsehoods
   - ◯ inclines

3. What is true of Lake Vostok?
   - ◯ It is completely frozen.
   - ◯ It is a saltwater lake.
   - ◯ It is beneath a thick slab of ice.
   - ◯ It is heated by the sun.

4. Which of the following is closest in meaning to frigid in paragraph 1?
   ◯ Extremely cold
   ◯ Never changing
   ◯ Quite harsh
   ◯ Rarely recorded

5. All of the following are true about the 1970 survey of Antarctica EXCEPT that it
   ◯ was conducted by air
   ◯ made use of radio waves
   ◯ did not measure the exact size of the lake
   ◯ was controlled by a satellite

6. It can be inferred from the passage that the ice would not be flat if
   ◯ there were no lake
   ◯ the lake were not so big
   ◯ Antarctica were not so cold
   ◯ radio waves were not used

7. The word microbes in paragraph 3 could best be replaced by which of the following?
   ◯ Pieces of dust
   ◯ Trapped bubbles
   ◯ Tiny organisms
   ◯ Rays of light

8. The passage mentions which of the following as a reason for the importance of Lake Vostok to scientists?
   ◯ It can be studied using radio waves.
   ◯ It may contain uncontaminated microbes.
   ◯ It may have elevated levels of ultraviolet light.
   ◯ It has already been contaminated.

9. The word downside in paragraph 3 is closest in meaning to
   ◯ bottom level
   ◯ negative aspect
   ◯ underside
   ◯ buried section

10. The paragraph following the passage most probably discusses
    ◯ further discoveries on the surface of Antarctica
    ◯ problems with satellite-borne radar equipment
    ◯ ways to study Lake Vostok without contaminating it
    ◯ the harsh climate of Antarctica

PASSAGE TWO (Questions 11-20)

During the heyday of the railroads, when America's rail system provided the bulk of the country's passenger and freight transportation, various types of railroad cars were in service to accomplish the varied tasks handled by the railroads. One type of car that was not available for public use prior to the Civil War, however, was a sleeping car; ideas for sleeping cars abounded at the time, but these ideas were unworkable. It unfortunately took the death of a president to make the sleeping car a viable reality.

Cabinet-maker George M. Pullman had recognized the demand for sleeping cars and had worked on developing experimental models of sleeping cars in the decade leading up to the Civil War. However, in spite of the fact that he had made successful test runs on the Chicago and Alton Railroads with his models, he was unable to sell his idea because his models were too wide and too high for existing train stations and bridges. In 1863, after spending time working as a storekeeper in a Colorado mining town, he invested his savings of twenty thousand dollars, a huge fortune at that time and all the money that he had in the world, in a luxurious sleeping car that he named the Pioneer. Pullman and friend Ben Field built the Pioneer on the site of the present-day Chicago Union Station. For two years, however, the Pioneer sat on a railroad siding, useless because it could not fit through train stations and over bridges.

Following President Lincoln's assassination in 1865, the state of Illinois, Lincoln's birthplace, wanted to transport the presidential casket in the finest fashion possible. The Pullman Pioneer was the most elegant car around; in order to make the Pullman part of the presidential funeral train in its run from Springfield to Chicago, the state cut down station platforms and raised bridges in order to accommodate the luxurious railway car. The Pullman car greatly impressed the funeral party, which included Lincoln's successor as president, General Ulysses S. Grant, and Grant later requested the Pioneer for a trip from Detroit to Chicago. To satisfy Grant's request for the Pioneer, the Michigan Central Railroad made improvements on its line to accommodate the wide car, and soon other railroads followed. George Pullman founded the Pullman Palace Car Company in partnership with financier Andrew Carnegie and eventually became a millionaire.

11. Which of the following best states the main idea of the passage?
     ◯ America's railroads used to provide much of the country's transportation.
     ◯ President Lincoln's assassination in 1865 shocked the nation.
     ◯ George Pullman was the only one to come up with the idea for a sleeping car.
     ◯ Pullman's idea for a sleeping car became workable after Lincoln's death.

12. A heyday in paragraph 1 is most probably a
     ◯ time for harvest
     ◯ a period with low prices
     ◯ a period of great success
     ◯ a type of railroad schedule

13. It can be inferred from the passage that before the Civil War, sleeping cars
     ◯ were used abundantly
     ◯ were thought to be a good idea
     ◯ were only used privately
     ◯ were used by presidents

14. The word test in paragraph 2 could best be replaced by which of the following?

   ◯ Exam
   ◯ Trial
   ◯ Inspection
   ◯ Scientific

15. What was the initial problem that made Pullman's cars unusable?

   ◯ They were too large.
   ◯ They were too expensive.
   ◯ They were too slow.
   ◯ They were too unusual.

16. What is stated in the passage about George Pullman?

   ◯ He never worked in a store.
   ◯ He always lived in Chicago.
   ◯ He worked in a mine.
   ◯ He saved money for his project.

17. The word site in paragraph 2 is closest in meaning to which of the following?

   ◯ Factory
   ◯ View
   ◯ Location
   ◯ Foundation

18. Why did the state of Illinois want to use the Pullman in Lincoln's funeral train?

   ◯ It was superior to other cars.
   ◯ It was the only railroad car that could make it from Springfield to Chicago.
   ◯ Ulysses S. Grant requested it.
   ◯ The Pullman Palace Car Company was a major Illinois business.

19. It can be inferred from the passage that the Michigan Central Railroad

   ◯ was owned by George Pullman
   ◯ controlled the railroad tracks between Detroit and Chicago
   ◯ was the only railroad company to accommodate wide cars
   ◯ was the sole manufacturer of the Pioneer

20. This passage would most likely be assigned in which of the following courses?

   ◯ Engineering
   ◯ Political science
   ◯ Finance
   ◯ History

Check your answers in the Answer Key on page 167.
Then turn to page 178 and circle the numbers of the questions that you missed.

Question Type 2: CLICK-ON QUESTIONS

Click-on questions are one of the three types of questions that may accompany a reading passage on the TOEFL® Computer-Based Test. In this type of question, you may be asked to click on a word, a sentence, a paragraph, or a drawing. The TOEFL® Computer-Based Test uses click-on questions to test **main ideas, vocabulary, pronoun reference,** or **details.**

In a click-on question, you are asked to click on a word, a sentence, a paragraph, or a drawing that contains the answer to a question. The following passage is accompanied by examples of the various types of click-on questions that you might encounter on the TOEFL® Computer-Based Test. The first question is a **vocabulary** question that asks you to find a word in the first paragraph with a specific meaning.

Example

You see part of the passage and the first question on the screen.

. . . .

You scroll through the passage for the answer.

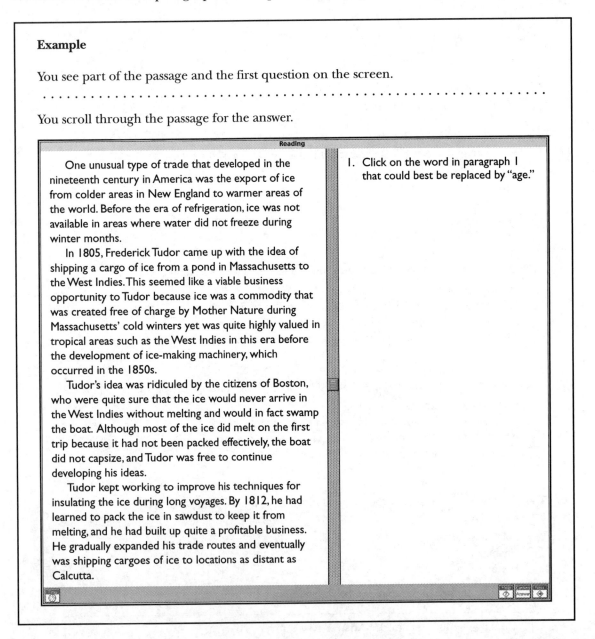

Reading

One unusual type of trade that developed in the nineteenth century in America was the export of ice from colder areas in New England to warmer areas of the world. Before the era of refrigeration, ice was not available in areas where water did not freeze during winter months.

In 1805, Frederick Tudor came up with the idea of shipping a cargo of ice from a pond in Massachusetts to the West Indies. This seemed like a viable business opportunity to Tudor because ice was a commodity that was created free of charge by Mother Nature during Massachusetts' cold winters yet was quite highly valued in tropical areas such as the West Indies in this era before the development of ice-making machinery, which occurred in the 1850s.

Tudor's idea was ridiculed by the citizens of Boston, who were quite sure that the ice would never arrive in the West Indies without melting and would in fact swamp the boat. Although most of the ice did melt on the first trip because it had not been packed effectively, the boat did not capsize, and Tudor was free to continue developing his ideas.

Tudor kept working to improve his techniques for insulating the ice during long voyages. By 1812, he had learned to pack the ice in sawdust to keep it from melting, and he had built up quite a profitable business. He gradually expanded his trade routes and eventually was shipping cargoes of ice to locations as distant as Calcutta.

1. Click on the word in paragraph 1 that could best be replaced by "age."

You click on the word *era* in the first paragraph.

. . . .

You click on Next .

. . . .

Another question appears on the screen.

To answer this question, you skim through the first paragraph looking for such a word. The second sentence of the first paragraph contains the expression *before the era of refrigeration,* and the word *era* could be replaced by *age* in this expression. To answer this question, you should click on *era*. Then, click on Next to move to the next question.

After you have clicked on Next , another question appears in the question box on the computer screen. The second question is a **detail** question that asks you to click on one of four drawings. Since the second question is most probably answered after the first question in the passage, you should scroll to the part of the passage that follows the answer to the first question and skim for information about *where Tudor obtained ice.*

You see part of the passage and the second question on the screen.

. . . .

You scroll through the passage for the answer.

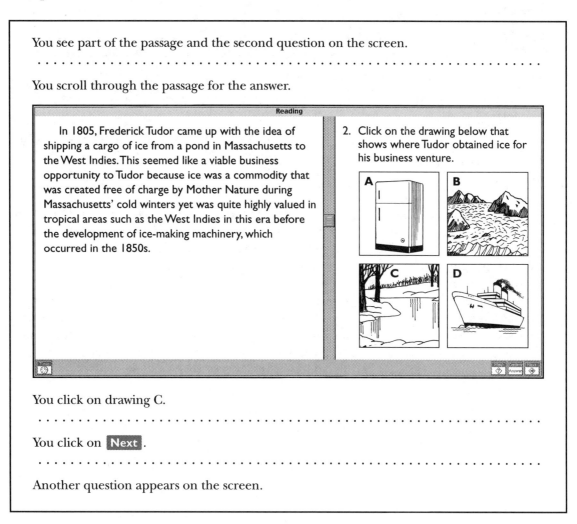

You click on drawing C.

. . . .

You click on Next .

. . . .

Another question appears on the screen.

After you have clicked on ▐Next▌ , a new question appears in the question box on the computer screen. The third question is a **pronoun reference** question that asks you to find the referent for the pronoun *it*. The pronoun *it* is highlighted in the passage. You should scroll to the part of the passage that includes the highlighted pronoun. Since a pronoun referent generally precedes the pronoun, you should look before the pronoun to find its referent.

You see part of the passage and the second question on the screen. The pronoun *it* is highlighted.

· ·

You scroll through the passage for the highlighted pronoun, if necessary.

Reading

Tudor's idea was ridiculed by the citizens of Boston, who were quite sure that the ice would never arrive in the West Indies without melting and would in fact swamp the boat. Although most of the ice did melt on the first trip because ▐it▌ had not been packed effectively, the boat did not capsize, and Tudor was free to continue developing his ideas.	3. Look at the word ▐it▌ in paragraph 3. Click on the word or phrase in paragraph 3 that ▐it▌ refers to.

You click on the word *ice* in the line before *it*.

· ·

You click on ▐Next▌ .

· ·

Another question appears on the screen.

The singular nouns that precede the singular pronoun *it* are *boat, ice,* and *trip.* You should try each of these nouns in the sentence in place of the pronoun *it;* since *ice...had not been packed effectively..., ice* is the best answer to this question. To answer this question, you should click on the word *ice* in the line before *it.* Then, click on ▐Next▌ to move to the next question.

After you have clicked on ▐Next▌ , another question appears on the screen. The fourth question is a **detail** question that asks you to click on the sentence that contains the answer to the question. Since the fourth question is most probably answered after the third question in the passage, you should scroll to the part of the passage that follows the answer to the third question and skim for information about a way *to keep the ice frozen.*

You see part of the passage and the fourth question on the screen.

· ·

You scroll through the passage for the answer.

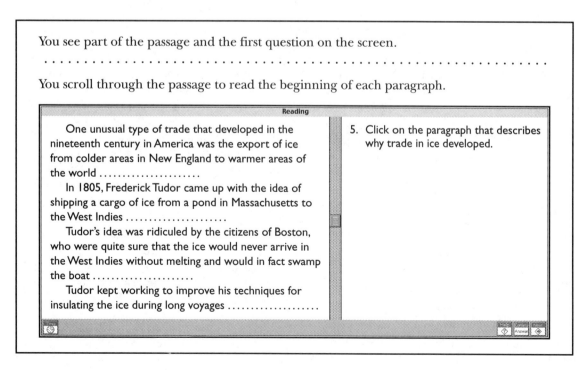

You click on the second sentence in the fourth paragraph.

· ·

You click on **Next** .

· ·

Another question appears on the screen.

The second sentence in the fourth paragraph states that Tudor *had learned to pack the ice in sawdust to keep it from melting,* so you should click on this sentence to answer the question. Then, click on **Next** to move to the next question.

After you have clicked on **Next** , a new question appears on the screen. The fifth question is a **main idea** question that asks you to click on the paragraph that develops a certain main idea. Since this is a **main idea** question, you should look at the first line of each paragraph to understand the main idea of each paragraph.

You see part of the passage and the first question on the screen.

· ·

You scroll through the passage to read the beginning of each paragraph.

> You click on the first paragraph.
>
> . . . .
>
> You click on `Next`.
>
> . . . .
>
> Another question appears on the screen.

The first sentence in the first paragraph mentions *trade that developed* and *the export of ice*. This paragraph most likely explains *why trade in ice developed*. You should click on the first paragraph to answer this question.

The following chart outlines the key information that you should remember about click-on questions on the TOEFL® Computer-Based Test:

THE CLICK-ON QUESTION	
WHAT IT TESTS	• a main idea • a directly answered detail • pronoun reference • vocabulary
HOW IT IS RELATED TO THE PAPER-AND-PENCIL TEST	It is a different type of question from what is found on the paper-and-pencil test. However, it tests many of the same skills as are found on the paper-and-pencil test.
HOW IT IS RELATED TO SKILLS IN *VOLUME A*	A number of the reading and vocabulary skills presented in *Volume A* are covered in the click-on questions on the TOEFL® Computer-Based Test: • Skills 1-2 (*Questions about the Ideas of a Passage*) • Skills 3-4 (*Directly Answered Questions*) • Skill 5 (*Pronoun Reference*) • Skills 8-11 (*Vocabulary Questions*)
WHERE ITS ANSWER CAN BE FOUND	For a **main idea** question, the answer can generally be determined by looking at the first sentence of each paragraph. For *other* types of questions, the answers are generally found in order in the passage.

HOW YOU SHOULD ANSWER IT	MAIN IDEA: 1. Choose a key idea from the question.
	  2. Look for this key idea in the first sentence of each paragraph.
	  3. Click on the paragraph that contains this key idea.

	DETAIL: 1. Choose a key word in the question.
	  2. Skim and scroll to the appropriate part of the passage for the key word or idea.
	  3. Read the sentence that contains the key word or idea carefully to see if it answers the question.
	  4. Click on the sentence that contains the answer, or click on the picture that depicts the answer.

PRONOUN:	1. Scroll to the pronoun in the passage. (The pronoun is highlighted in the passage.) 2. Look for nouns that come before the pronoun. 3. Try each of the nouns in the sentence in place of the pronoun. 4. Choose the noun that makes the most sense in the sentence, and click on that noun.
VOCABULARY:	1. For some vocabulary questions, the vocabulary word is highlighted in the passage. Scroll to the vocabulary word in the passage. 2. Read the context around the vocabulary word, and try the answers in place of the vocabulary word in the passage. 3. For other vocabulary questions, the paragraph where the word is found is mentioned in the question. Skim the paragraph looking for an appropriate synonym (or antonym). 4. Try the vocabulary word in various contexts in the passage until you find a context that fits.

Exercise: CLICK-ON QUESTIONS

Study each of the passages and answer the questions that follow. In this exercise, each passage is followed by a number of click-on questions of the type that you might find on the TOEFL® Computer-Based Test. (On the actual TOEFL® Computer-Based Test, the click-on questions are intermixed with the other types of questions, and only one highlight appears in a passage at a time.)

PASSAGE ONE (Questions 1-11)

In the first half of the 19th century, the U.S. government decided that it needed to set up a system for protecting its coastline. It then began building a series of forts along the coast of the eastern part of the country to facilitate its defenses.

The largest of these forts was Fort Jefferson, which was begun in 1846. This fort was built on Garden Key, one of a cluster of small coral islands 70 miles west of Key West. At the time of its construction, Fort Jefferson was believed to be of primary strategic importance to the United States because of its location at the entryway to the Gulf of Mexico. Because of its location at the entrance to a great body of water, it became known as the Gibraltar of the Gulf, in reference to the island located at the mouth of the Mediterranean. The fort itself was a massive structure. It was hexagonal in shape, with 8-foot-thick walls, and was surrounded by a medieval-style moat for added security. Covering most of the Garden Key, it was approximately half a mile in circumference.

In the latter half of the 19th century, during the Civil War and its aftermath, the fort was used as a prison rather than a military installation. The most notorious of its prisoners was Dr. Samuel Mudd, a physician who was most probably innocently involved in the assassination of Abraham Lincoln. The actual assassin, John Wilkes Booth, broke his leg as he lept from the stage of the Ford Theater during the assassination. Dr. Mudd set Booth's broken leg, unaware of Booth's involvement in the assassination. As a result of this action, Dr. Mudd was sentenced to life in prison and remanded to Fort Jefferson. He was pardoned after only four years because of his courageous efforts in combatting an epidemic of yellow fever that ravaged the fort.

Continuous use of Fort Jefferson ended in the 1870s, although the U.S. Navy continued with sporadic use of it into the 20th century. Today, the massive ruins still remain on the tiny island that stands guard over the entrance to the gulf, undisturbed except for the occasional sightseer who ventures out from the coast to visit.

1. Click on the word in paragraph 1 that could best be replaced by "chain."

2. Click on the sentence in paragraph 2 that mentions what makes up the island where Fort Jefferson is located.

3. Click on the drawing that shows the location of Fort Jefferson.

4. Look at the word it in paragraph 2. Click on the word or phrase in paragraph 2 that it refers to.

5. Click on the drawing that represents Fort Jefferson and Garden Key.

6. Click on the sentence in paragraph 3 that describes an injury to the man who shot Lincoln.

7. Look at the word latter in paragraph 3. Click on another word or expression in paragraph 1 that is opposite in meaning to latter.

8. Look at the word He in paragraph 3. Click on the word or phrase in paragraph 3 that He refers to.

9. Click on the paragraph that describes the use of Fort Jefferson as a penal institution.

10. Look at the word Continuous in paragraph 4. Click on another word or phrase in paragraph 4 that is opposite in meaning to Continuous.

11. Click on the paragraph that describes the current condition of Fort Jefferson.

PASSAGE TWO (Questions 12-23)

Mutualism is a type of symbiosis that occurs when two unlike organisms live together in a state that is mutually beneficial. It can exist between two animals, between two plants, or between a plant and an animal. Mutualism is unlike the symbiotic state of commensalism in that commensalism is a one-sided state in which a host gives and a guest takes, while in mutualism both partners live on a give-and-take basis.

In the African wilds, the zebra and the ostrich enjoy a symbiotic relationship that enhances the ability of each of these large land animals to survive. Both serve as prey for the lion, and neither has the capability alone to withstand an attack from this fierce hunter. However, when the zebra and the ostrich collaborate in their defense by alerting each other to possible danger from an approaching predator, the lion is rarely able to capture more than the oldest or feeblest of the herd.

The complementary physical strengths and weaknesses of the ostrich and the zebra allow them to work in coordination to avoid succumbing to the lion. The ostrich, the largest flightless bird in the world, possesses great speed and keen eyesight, which enable it to spot large predatory animals long before they are able to position themselves to attack. The zebra, with a running speed equal to that of the ostrich, has excellent hearing and a good sense of smell but lacks the sharp eyesight of the ostrich. When ostriches and zebras intermix for grazing, each animal benefits from the ability of the other to detect approaching danger. If either animal senses danger, both animals are alerted and take off. With the running speed that both of these animals possess, they are able to outrun any predator except the cheetah.

12. Click on the word in the paragraph 1 that is closest in meaning to "advantageous."

13. Click on the sentence in paragraph 1 that mentions the various types of pairs of living organisms that can maintain mutualistic relationships.

14. Click on the drawing that describes a commensalist state.

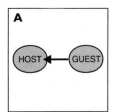 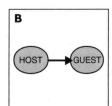 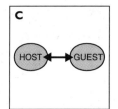

15. Click on the paragraph that describes the difference between two different types of symbiotic states.

16. Look at the word hunter in paragraph 2. Click on another word or phrase in paragraph 2 that is close in meaning to hunter.

17. Click on the word or phrase in paragraph 2 that is closest in meaning to "work together."

18.   Look at the word it in paragraph 3. Click on the word or phrase in paragraph 3 that it refers to.

19.   Look at the word that in paragraph 3. Click on the word or phrase in paragraph 3 that that refers to.

20.   Look at the word sharp in paragraph 3. Click on another word or phrase in paragraph 3 that is close in meaning to sharp.

21.   Click on the drawing that describes what happens when a lion approaches a zebra and an ostrich.

   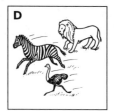

22.   Click on the sentence in paragraph 3 that mentions the one animal that is faster than both the ostrich and the zebra.

23.   Click on the paragraph that describes the relative abilities and deficiencies of zebras and ostriches.

Check your answers in the Answer Key on page 167.
Then turn to page 178 and circle the numbers of the questions that you missed.

Question Type 3: INSERTION QUESTIONS

Insertion questions are one of the three types of questions that may accompany a reading passage on the TOEFL® Computer-Based Test. The TOEFL® Computer-Based Test uses insertion questions to test your ability to recognize whether a given piece of information is a **main idea,** a **supporting detail** or **example,** a **conclusion** or a **transition.** After you determine the type of information, you must indicate where this piece of information fits into a passage.

In an insertion question, you are asked to click on a square in the passage to indicate that a given piece of information should be inserted in that position. The following passages are accompanied by examples of various types of insertion questions that you might encounter on the TOEFL® Computer-Based Test. The first passage is accompanied by examples of the insertion of a **supporting detail** and a **conclusion.**

Example I

You see part of the passage and the first question on the computer screen. Each answer choice is marked with a square (■). You may not be able to see all the answer choices at once.

. . . .

You scroll through the passage to see each answer choice.

Reading	
Thunderstorms, with their regular accompaniments of lightning, hail, downbursts, and heavy rainfall, have a notorious potential for causing massive amounts of destruction. ■ The lightning associated with thunderstorms causes several hundred million dollars of property damage, in the neighborhood of two hundred deaths, and thousands of forest fires in the United States alone. ■ The hail that can accompany thunderstorms also causes several million dollars worth of damage to crops and other personal property. ■ In addition to the hail and lightning associated with thunderstorms, downbursts are also potentially quite dangerous. ■ A final problem associated with thunderstorms is the heavy localized rainfall that can occur when a powerful storm remains relatively stationary and dumps a large amount of water over a limited space; when this occurs in areas that are geographically prone to it, flash floods can and do occur. ■	1. The following sentence could be added to the passage. **Downbursts are intense, downward-moving drafts with wind speeds in excess of 80 meters per second.** Where would it best fit in the passage? Click on the square (■) to add the sentence to the passage.

You click on the square between *quite dangerous* and *A final problem.*

. . . .

You click on Next .

. . . .

Another question appears on the screen.

To answer this question, you should first read the sentence and notice that this sentence discusses *downbursts.* Then you should look at the passage and should notice from the first sentence of the passage that the passage is about thunderstorms and that four *accompaniments* of thunderstorms, including *downbursts,* are discussed. This indicates that the sentence to be inserted describes one of the **supporting details** about the topic *thunderstorms.* Next, you should scroll and skim through the passage looking for the four supporting details. The passage mentions first *lightning,* then *hail,* then *downbursts,* and finally *heavy rainfall.* The additional information about *downbursts* should therefore be inserted after *downbursts* are first mentioned. To answer this question, you should click on the square between *quite dangerous* and *A final problem.* Then, click on Next to move to the next question.

After you have clicked on Next , another question appears on the computer screen. This question asks you to insert another sentence into the passage. To answer this question, you should first read the sentence to determine the type of information given in the sentence.

You see part of the passage and the second question on the computer screen. Each answer choice is marked with a square (■). You may not be able to see all the answer choices at once.

. . . .

You scroll through the passage to see each answer choice.

Reading

Thunderstorms, with their regular accompaniments of lightning, hail, downbursts, and heavy rainfall, have a notorious potential for causing massive amounts of destruction. ■ The lightning associated with thunderstorms causes several hundred million dollars of property damage, in the neighborhood of two hundred deaths, and thousands of forest fires in the United States alone. ■ The hail that can accompany thunderstorms also causes several million dollars worth of damage to crops and other personal property. ■ In addition to the hail and lightning associated with thunderstorms, downbursts are also potentially quite dangerous. ■ A final problem associated with thunderstorms is the heavy localized rainfall that can occur when a powerful storm remains relatively stationary and dumps a large amount of water over a limited space; when this occurs in areas that are geographically prone to it, flash floods can and do occur. ■

2. The following sentence could be added to the passage.

Because of all these potentially dangerous factors related to thunderstorms, these storms are not to be taken lightly.

Where would it best fit in the passage? Click on the square (■) to add the sentence to the passage.

You click on the square at the end of the passage.

. . . .

You click on Next .

. . . .

Another question appears on the screen.

As you read the sentence, you should notice that this sentence mentions *all these...factors* and states that *these storms are not to be taken lightly.* Because the idea that the storms should not be taken lightly is a possible inference or result that can be drawn from the supporting details in the passage about all of the damage caused by each factor, this sentence is a **conclusion** that belongs at the end of the passage, after a discussion of each of the factors. To answer this question, you should click on the square at the end of the passage to indicate that this sentence should be added there. Then, click on **Next** to move to the next question.

The next passage is accompanied by examples of the insertion of a **main idea** and a **transition.**

Example II

You see part of the passage and the first question on the computer screen. Each answer choice is marked with a square (■). You may not be able to see all the answer choices at once.

. . . .

You scroll through the passage to see each answer choice.

Reading

■ Most tall buildings in the United States, for example, do not have a thirteenth floor, and airplanes often bypass a thirteenth row. ■ In addition, many towns will give the street between 12th and 14th a name other than 13th. ■ Fear of the number thirteen has even been accorded its own name in psychological jargon: triskaidekaphobia. ■

The reason for the esteem that the United States holds for the number thirteen is that the United States consisted of thirteen colonies at its inception. The seal of the United States, found on the back of the modern dollar bill, includes thirteen stars and thirteen stripes as well as a bald eagle holding thirteen arrows in one claw and a laurel branch with thirteen leaves and thirteen berries in the other. This abundant use of the number thirteen in the seal of the United States, of course, commemorates the country's thirteen original colonies.

1. The following sentence could be added to paragraph 1.

   The number thirteen has long been regarded as an omen of misfortune, and examples of the negative superstition attached to this number abound.

   Where would it best fit in the paragraph? Click on the square (■) to add the sentence to the paragraph.

You click on the square at the beginning of the first paragraph.

. . . .

You click on **Next**.

. . . .

Another question appears on the screen.

The first question asks you to insert a sentence into the first paragraph of the passage. First, you should read the sentence, and you should see that it mentions *examples of the negative superstition.* Then, you should look at the first paragraph and concentrate on the type of information included in each of the sentences. In the first paragraph, there are various examples of negative superstitions about the number thirteen: in *tall buildings,* in *airplanes,* and in *street numbers*. From this, you can determine that the sentence to be inserted is a **topic** or **main idea** sentence and should be inserted at the beginning of the paragraph. To answer this question, you should click on the square at the beginning of the first paragraph. Then, click on Next to move to the next question.

After you have clicked on Next, another question appears in the question box on the computer screen. The second question asks you to insert a sentence into the second paragraph of the passage.

You see part of the passage and the second question on the computer screen. Each answer choice is marked with a box (■). You may not be able to see all the answer choices at once.

. . . .

You scroll through the passage to see each answer choice.

> **Reading**
>
> ■ The reason for the esteem that the United States holds for the number thirteen is that the United States consisted of thirteen colonies at its inception. ■ The seal of the United States, found on the back of the modern dollar bill, includes thirteen stars and thirteen stripes as well as a bald eagle holding thirteen arrows in one claw and a laurel branch with thirteen leaves and thirteen berries in the other. ■ This abundant use of the number thirteen in the seal of the United States, of course, commemorates the country's thirteen original colonies. ■
>
> 2. The following sentence could be added to paragraph 2.
>
> **Even though American culture contains numerous examples of its tradition of suspicion of the misfortunes caused by the number thirteen, this number is also held in high esteem.**
>
> Where would it best fit in the paragraph? Click on the square (■) to add the sentence to the paragraph.

You click on the square at the beginning of the second paragraph.

. . . .

You click on Next.

. . . .

Another question appears on the screen.

First, you should read the sentence carefully, and you should note that there are two parts to this sentence: the first part mentions the *tradition of suspicion*, and the second part mentions *high esteem*. Next, you should look at the passage and see that the first line of the second paragraph discusses *esteem...for the number thirteen*, and you should also remember that the first paragraph discussed the *misfortune* attached to the number thirteen. From this, you can determine that the sentence to be inserted is a **transition** sentence that relates the ideas of the first paragraph to the ideas of the second paragraph. Because this sentence serves as a transition between the two paragraphs, it may be placed at the beginning of the second paragraph. To answer this question, you should click on the square at the beginning of the second paragraph. Then, click on Next to move to the next question.

The following chart outlines the key information that you should remember about insertion questions on the TOEFL® Computer-Based Test:

THE INSERTION QUESTION	
WHAT IT TESTS	• identification of the type of information (i.e., *main idea, detail, conclusion, transition*) • insertion of the information into the appropriate place in a passage
HOW IT IS RELATED TO THE PAPER-AND-PENCIL TEST	It is a different type of question from what is found on the paper-and-pencil test. The language skills in this type of question are generally not covered on the paper-and-pencil test.
HOW IT IS RELATED TO SKILLS IN *VOLUME A*	The language skills covered in the insertion questions are not covered in *Volume A*.
WHERE ITS ANSWER CAN BE FOUND	The answers to these questions are generally found in order in the passage.
HOW YOU SHOULD ANSWER IT	1. Preview the first line of each paragraph of the passage to determine the overall organization of ideas. 2. Look in the sentence to be inserted for any transitional words or expressions *(i.e., however, as a result)* that might indicate the type of information included in the sentence. 3. Read the sentence to be inserted into the passage, and determine what type of information it is (i.e., *main idea, detail, transition,* or *conclusion*). 4. Study each of the answer choice squares to determine where the sentence should be inserted. Click on the best choice.

Exercise: INSERTION QUESTIONS

Study each of the passages and answer the questions that follow. In this exercise, each passage is followed by a number of insertion questions of the type that you might find on the TOEFL® Computer-Based Test. The answer choices are indicated with lettered boxes. (On the actual TOEFL® Computer-Based Test, the insertion questions are intermixed with the other types of questions, and the answer choices are indicated with solid boxes.)

PASSAGE ONE (Questions 1-2)

[1A] One method of popping corn involved skewering an ear of corn on a stick and roasting it until kernels popped off the ear. **[1B]** Corn was also popped by first cutting the kernels off the cob, throwing them into a fire, and gathering them as they popped out of the fire. **[1C]** In a final method for popping corn, sand and unpopped kernels of corn were mixed together in a cooking pot and heated until the corn popped to the surface of the sand in the pot. **[1D]**

[2A] This traditional Native American dish was quite a novelty to newcomers to the Americas. **[2B]** Columbus and his sailors found natives in the West Indies wearing popcorn necklaces, and explorer Hernando Cortes described the use of popcorn amulets in the religious ceremonies of the Aztecs. **[2C]** According to legendary descriptions of this celebratory meal, Quadequina, the brother of Chief Massasoit, contributed several deerskin bags of popcorn to the celebration. **[2D]**

1. The following sentence could be added to paragraph 1.

   Native Americans have been popping corn for at least five thousand years, using a variety of different methods.

   Where would it best fit in the paragraph? Click on the square (■) to add the sentence to the paragraph.

2. The following sentence could be added to paragraph 2.

   A century after these early explorers, the Pilgrims at Plymouth may have been introduced to popcorn at the first Thanksgiving dinner.

   Where would it best fit in the paragraph? Click on the square (■) to add the sentence to the paragraph.

PASSAGE TWO (Questions 3-5)

3A The aurora are a phenomenal display of greenish-white light typically visible in the skies above the polar regions of the Earth. **3B** This natural light show constantly changes in configuration and can shift dramatically in seconds. **3C**

4A Richard Carrington, an English physicist and astronomer, was the first person to determine the actual cause of the aurora. **4B** On September 1, 1859, Carrington observed a tremendous solar flare on the surface of the Sun. **4C** Carrington came to the conclusion that the huge solar flares two nights earlier had played a role. **4D** Carrington's first hunch has since been scientifically established. **4E** It is now known that the solar wind, a continuous flow of charged subatomic particles from the Sun that streams around the Earth, causes the aurora as it passes through the Earth's geomagnetic field. **4F**

5A The aurora are generally a polar phenomenon; however, particularly strong aurora have at times appeared over densely populated areas of the Earth and have wreaked havoc. **5B** The 1859 aurora noted by Carrington took out telegraph communication throughout much of Europe by overwhelming the pulses of electromagnets. **5C** A century later, in 1958, a tremendous auroral storm above North America overloaded utility circuits and caused a blackout in much of northeastern Canada. **5D** Twenty auroral superstorms have been recorded since 1880, and human dependence on electrical devices has been increasing steadily. **5E**

3. The following sentence could be added to paragraph 1.

   It may change from a barely visible glow to blinding sheets of swaying, shimmering light.

   Where would it best fit in the paragraph? Click on the square (■) to add the sentence to the paragraph.

4. The following sentence could be added to paragraph 2.

   Two nights later, an intense aurora spread over large parts of Europe.

   Where would it best fit in the paragraph? Click on the square (■) to add the sentence to the paragraph.

5. The following sentence could be added to paragraph 3.

   With this large number of superstorms and ever-widening use of electrical devices, further auroral interference into the lives of humanity seems likely.

   Where would it best fit in the paragraph? Click on the square (■) to add the sentence to the paragraph.

PASSAGE THREE (Questions 6-8)

A number of nonmetric measurements in common use may at first glance seem to lack the logic and clarity of the metric system, with its measurements all neatly based on tens and multiples of tens. However, these nonmetric measurements developed over time from habitual use of commonplace items to make simple measurements. They might not seem like simple measurements today, but such is their history.

6A As can be inferred from the name, the Romans used the term *foot* to describe the length of a man's foot, from the base of the heel to the tip of the big toe. **6B** Though not exactly an accurate measurement, due to the varying lengths of men's feet, a foot was a measurement that was easy to conceptualize and visualize by most people. **6C** The term *yard* was used extensively by the English as the measurement from the tip of a man's nose to the tip of his outstretched thumb. **6D** English King Edward I redefined a yard as equivalent to three feet in 1305. **6E**

7A The word *mile* comes from the Latin word *mille,* which means *one thousand.* **7B** A mile was meant to conform to a distance of one thousand paces, each pace consisting of two steps or approximately five thousand feet. **7C**

8A On the ocean, speed is measured in knots, with one knot roughly equivalent to one nautical mile per hour. **8B** This measurement of speed comes from the days when sailors used a knotted rope to determine their speed while at sea. **8C** A rope was knotted at regular intervals and tossed overboard. **8D** The rope was let out as sand flowed through an hour glass. **8E**

6. The following sentence could be added to paragraph 2.

   The measurements *foot* and *yard* developed based on average lengths of body parts.

   Where would it best fit in the paragraph? Click on the square (■) to add the sentence to the paragraph.

7. The following sentence could be added to paragraph 3.

   To describe longer distances, the Romans also invented the use of the term *mile.*

   Where would it best fit in the paragraph? Click on the square (■) to add the sentence to the paragraph.

8. The following sentence could be added to paragraph 4.

   When the sand had passed through the hour glass, the speed of the boat was determined by counting the number of knots that had been let out.

   Where would it best fit in the paragraph? Click on the square (■) to add the sentence to the paragraph.

PASSAGE FOUR (Questions 9-11)

9A In 1873, P.T. Barnum built Barnum's Monster Classical and Geological Hippodrome at the corner of Madison Avenue and 26th Street, across from Madison Square Park. **9B** Two years later, bandleader Patrick Gilmore bought the property, added statues and fountains, and renamed it Gilmore's Gardens. **9C** When Cornelius Vanderbuilt bought the property in 1879, it was renamed Madison Square Garden. **9D**

A second very lavish Madison Square Garden was built in the same location in 1890, with a ballroom, a restaurant, a theater, a rooftop garden, and a main arena with seating for 15,000. However, this elaborate Madison Square Garden lasted only until 1924, when it was torn down to make way for a forty-story skyscraper.

10A This new Madison Square Garden was constructed in a different location, on 8th Avenue and 50th Street and quite some distance from Madison Square Park and Madison Avenue. **10B** Rickard's Madison Square Garden served primarily as an arena for boxing prizefights and circus events until it outgrew its usefulness by the late 1950s. **10C**

11A A new location was found for a fourth Madison Square Garden, atop Pennsylvania Station, and plans were announced for its construction in 1960. **11B** This current edifice, which includes a huge sports arena, a bowling center, a 5,000-seat amphitheater, and a twenty-nine story office building, does retain the traditional name Madison Square Garden. **11C** The building is not located near Madison Square, nor does it have the flowery gardens that contributed to the original name. **11D**

9. The following sentence could be added to paragraph 1.

   Madison Square Garden, a world-famous sporting venue in New York City, has actually been a series of buildings in varied locations rather than a single building in one spot.

   Where would it best fit in the paragraph? Click on the square (■) to add the sentence to the paragraph.

10. The following sentence could be added to paragraph 3.

    When the second Madison Square Garden had been replaced in its location across from Madison Square Park, boxing promoter Tex Rickard raised six million dollars to build a new Madison Square Garden.

    Where would it best fit in the paragraph? Click on the square (■) to add the sentence to the paragraph.

11. The following sentence could be added to paragraph 4.

    However, the name is actually quite a misnomer.

    Where would it best fit in the paragraph? Click on the square (■) to add the sentence to the paragraph.

Check your answers in the Answer Key on page 167.
Then turn to page 178 and circle the numbers of the questions that you missed.

TOEFL® Computer-Based Test: THE READING SECTION

> The following test shows you what the Reading section of the TOEFL® Computer-Based Test looks like. On the CBT, you may be asked to complete forty-four questions in seventy minutes (or you may have a longer version of the test). The Reading section is linear rather than adaptive (the passages get progressively more difficult, and the order of the questions is based on the location of the answers in the passage).

DIRECTIONS: Study each of the passages and answer the questions that follow.

PASSAGE ONE (Questions 1-11)

Aspirin's origins go back at least as early as 1758. In that year, Englishman Edward Stone noticed a distinctive bitter flavor in the bark of the willow tree. **6A** To Stone, this particular bark seemed to have much in common with "Peruvian Bark," which had been used medicinally since the 1640s to bring down fevers and to treat malaria. **6B** Stone decided to test the effectiveness of the willow bark. **6C** He obtained some, pulverized it into tiny pieces, and conducted experiments on its properties. **6D** In 1763, Stone presented his findings to the British Royal Society.

Several decades later, further studies on the medicinal value of the willow bark were being conducted by two Italian scientists. These chemists, Brugnatelli and Fontana, determined that the active chemical that was responsible for the medicinal characteristics in the willow bark was the chemical salicin, which is the active ingredient of today's aspirin.

The name "aspirin" is the trade name of the drug based on the chemical salicin, properly known as acetylsalicylic acid. The trade name "aspirin" was invented for the drug in the 1890s by the Bayer Drug Company in Germany. The first bottles of aspirin actually went on sale to the public just prior to the turn of the century, in 1899.

1. According to the passage, aspirin originated
   ◯ no later than 1758
   ◯ sometime after 1758
   ◯ definitely sometime in 1758
   ◯ no earlier than 1758

2. It can be inferred from the passage that Peruvian Bark
   ◯ caused fevers
   ◯ was ineffective in treating malaria
   ◯ was described to the British Royal Society by Stone
   ◯ was in use prior to aspirin

3. Look at the word it in paragraph 1. Click on the word or phrase in paragraph 1 that it refers to.

4. Look at the word properties in paragraph 1. Click on another word in paragraph 2 that is close in meaning to properties.

5. Click on the drawing below that most clearly resembles the willow bark after Stone prepared it for his experiments.

 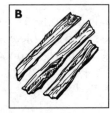 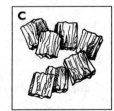 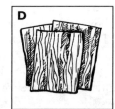

6. The following sentence could be added to paragraph 1.

    His tests demonstrated that this pulverized willow bark was effective both in reducing high temperatures and in relieving aches and pains.

    Where would it best fit in the paragraph? Click on the square (■) to add the sentence to the paragraph.

7. The Italian chemists mentioned in the passage most probably conducted their studies on willow bark
    ◯ in the 1750s
    ◯ in the 1760s
    ◯ in the 1770s
    ◯ in the 1780s

8. What is true about Brugnatelli and Fontana?
    ◯ They were from England.
    ◯ They added a chemical to the willow bark.
    ◯ They conducted studies on the willow bark.
    ◯ They were medical doctors.

9. Click on the sentence in paragraph 3 that names the scientific compound that makes up aspirin.

10. Click on the word or phrase in paragraph 3 that is opposite in meaning to "after."

11. Look at the word turn in paragraph 3. This word could best be replaced by
    ◯ spin
    ◯ corner
    ◯ change
    ◯ reversal

PASSAGE TWO (*Questions 12-21*)

Today, the most universally known style of trousers for both men and women is jeans; these trousers are worn throughout the world on a variety of occasions and in diverse situations. Also called levis or denims, jeans have an interesting history, one that is intermixed with the derivations of the words *jeans*, *denims*, and *levis*.

The word *jeans* is derived from the name of the place where a similar style of pants developed. In the sixteenth century, sailors from Genoa, Italy, wore a rather unique type of cotton trousers. In the French language, the word for the city of Genoa and for the people from that city is Genes; this name became attached to the specific style of pants worn by the sailors from this city and developed into the word *jeans* that today describes the descendents of the Genovese sailors' cotton pants.

Similar to the word *jeans*, the word *denim* is also derived from a place name. In the seventeenth century, French tailors began making trousers out of a specialized type of cloth that was developed in the city of Nimes, France, and was known as *serge de Nimes*. This name for the cloth underwent some transformations, and it eventually developed into today's *denim*, the material from which jeans are made and an alternate name for these popular pants.

The word *levis* came from the name of a person rather than a place. **20A** In the nineteenth century, immigrant Levi Strauss came to America and tried his hand at selling heavy canvas to miners taking part in the hunt for gold in northern California. **20B** This first endeavor was a failure, but Strauss later found success when he used the heavy canvas to make indestructible pants for the miners. **20C** Levi then switched the fabric from brown canvas to blue denim, creating a style of pants that long outlived him and today is referred to by his name. **20D** A modern-day urban shopper out to buy some levis is searching for a close relative of the product that Strauss had developed years earlier. **20E**

12. This passage is developed by
    ○ citing an effect and its causes
    ○ explaining history with three specific cases
    ○ demonstrating the sides of an issue
    ○ developing the biography of a famous person chronologically

13. Look at the word unique in paragraph 2. This word is closest in meaning to
    ○ universal
    ○ solitary
    ○ unusual
    ○ commonplace

14. All of the following are mentioned in the passage about Genoa EXCEPT that it
    ○ was the source of the word *jeans*
    ○ is in Italy
    ○ has a different name in the French language
    ○ is a landlocked city

15. Click on the word in paragraph 2 that is closest in meaning to "offspring."

16. The word *denim* was most probably derived from
     ◯ two French words
     ◯ two Italian words
     ◯ one French word and one Italian word
     ◯ three French words

17. Look at the word it in paragraph 3. Click on the word or phrase in paragraph 3 that it refers to.

18. Look at the word failure in paragraph 4. Click on another word or phrase in paragraph 4 that is opposite in meaning to failure.

19. Click on the word in paragraph 4 that is closest in meaning to "survived."

20. The following sentence could be added to paragraph 4.

     Strauss intended for this canvas to be used by miners to make heavy-duty tents.

     Where would it best fit in the paragraph? Click on the square (■) to add the sentence to the paragraph.

21. It can be inferred from the passage that, in order to develop the pants for which he became famous, Strauss did which of the following?
     ◯ He studied tailoring in Nimes.
     ◯ He used an existing type of material.
     ◯ He experimented with brown denim.
     ◯ He tested the pants for destructability.

PASSAGE THREE (Questions 22-33)

Thunderstorms, with their jagged bursts of lightning and roaring thunder, are actually one of nature's primary mechanisms for transferring heat from the surface of the earth into the atmosphere. A thunderstorm starts when low-lying pockets of warm air from the surface of the earth begin to rise. The pockets of warm air float upward through the air above that is both cooler and heavier. 25A The rising pockets cool as their pressure decreases, and their latent heat is released above the condensation line through the formation of cumulus clouds. 25B

What will happen with these clouds depends on the temperature of the atmosphere. 25C In winter, the air temperature differential between higher and lower altitudes is not extremely great, and the temperature of the rising air mass drops more slowly. 25D In summer, however, when there is a high accumulation of heat near the earth's surface, in direct contrast to the considerably colder air higher up, the temperature differential between higher and lower altitudes is much more pronounced. 25E As warm air rises in this type of environment, the temperature drops much more rapidly than it does in winter; when the temperature drops more than four degrees Fahrenheit per thousand feet of altitude, cumulus clouds aggregate into a single massive cumulonimbus cloud, or thunderhead.

In isolation, a single thunderstorm is an impressive but fairly benign way for Mother Earth to defuse trapped heat from her surface; thunderstorms, however, can appear in concert, and the resulting show, while extremely impressive, can also prove extraordinarily destructive. When there is a large-scale collision between cold air and warm air masses during the summer months, a squall line, or series of thunderheads, may develop. It is common for a squall line to begin when an advancing cold front meets up with and forces itself under a layer of warm and moist air, creating a line of thunderstorms that races forward at speeds of approximately forty miles per hour. A squall line, which can be hundreds of miles long and can contain fifty distinct thunderheads, is a magnificent force of nature with incredible potential for destruction. Within the squall line, often near its southern end, can be found supercells, long-lived rotating storms of exceptional strength that serve as the source of tornadoes.

22. The topic of the passage is
     ⭕ the development of thunderstorms and squall lines
     ⭕ the devastating effects of tornadoes
     ⭕ cumulus and cumulonimbus clouds
     ⭕ the power of tornadoes

23. Look at the word mechanisms in paragraph 1. They are most likely
     ⭕ machines
     ⭕ motions
     ⭕ methods
     ⭕ materials

24. Click on the sentence in paragraph 1 that indicates where cumulus clouds form.

25. The following sentence could be added to the passage.

     During these colder months, the atmosphere, therefore, tends to remain rather stable.

     Where would it best fit in the passage? Click on the square (■) to add the sentence to the passage.

26. It can be inferred from the passage that, in summer,

   ◯ there is not a great temperature differential between higher and lower altitudes
   ◯ the greater temperature differential between higher and lower altitudes makes thunderstorms more likely to occur
   ◯ there is not much cold air higher up in the atmosphere
   ◯ the temperature of rising air drops more slowly than it does in winter

27. Look at the word benign in paragraph 3. Click on another word in paragraph 3 that is opposite in meaning to benign.

28. Look at the expression in concert in paragraph 3. This expression could best be replaced by

   ◯ as a chorus
   ◯ with other musicians
   ◯ as a cluster
   ◯ in a performance

29. Click on the drawing below that most closely resembles a squall line.

30. Look at the word itself in paragraph 3. Click on the word or phrase in paragraph 3 that itself refers to.

31. All of the following are mentioned in the passage about supercells EXCEPT that they

   ◯ are of short duration
   ◯ have circling winds
   ◯ have extraordinary power
   ◯ can give birth to tornadoes

32. This reading would most probably be assigned in which of the following courses?

   ◯ Geology
   ◯ Meteorology
   ◯ Marine Biology
   ◯ Chemistry

33. The paragraph following the passage most likely discusses

   ◯ the lightning and thunder associated with thunderstorms
   ◯ various types of cloud formations
   ◯ the forces that contribute to the formation of squall lines
   ◯ the development of tornadoes within supercells

It is often the case with folktales that they develop from actual happenings but in their development lose much of their factual base; the story of Pocahontas quite possibly fits into this category of folktale. This princess of the Powhatan tribe was firmly established in the lore of early America and has been made even more famous by the Disney film based on the folktale that arose from her life. She was a real-life person, but the actual story of her life most probably differed considerably from the folktale and the movie based on the folktale.

Powhatan, the chief of a confederacy of tribes in Virginia, had several daughters, none of whom was actually named Pocahontas. The nickname means "playful one," and several of Powhatan's daughters were called Pocahontas. The daughter of Powhatan who became the subject of the folktale was named Matoaka. What has been verified about Matoaka, or Pocahontas as she has come to be known, is that she did marry an Englishman and that she did spend time in England before she died there at a young age. In the spring of 1613, a young Pocahontas was captured by the English and taken to Jamestown. There she was treated with courtesy as the daughter of chief Powhatan. While Pocahontas was at Jamestown, English gentleman John Rolfe fell in love with her and asked her to marry. Both the governor of the Jamestown colony and Pocahontas's father Powhatan approved the marriage as a means of securing peace between Powhatan's tribe and the English at Jamestown. In 1616, Pocahontas accompanied her new husband to England, where she was royally received. Shortly before her planned return to Virginia in 1617, she contracted an illness and died rather suddenly.

44A A major part of the folktale of Pocahontas that is unverified concerns her love for English Captain John Smith in the period of time before her capture by the British and her rescue of him from almost certain death. **44B** Captain John Smith was indeed at the colony of Jamestown and was acquainted with Powhatan and his daughters; he even described meeting them in a 1612 journal. **44C** However, the story of his rescue by the young maiden did not appear in his writings until 1624, well after Pocahontas had aroused widespread interest in England by her marriage to an English gentleman and her visit to England. **44D** It is this discrepancy in dates that has caused some historians to doubt the veracity of the tale. **44E**

34. The main idea of the passage is that
   ◯ folktales are often not very factual
   ◯ Pocahontas did not really exist
   ◯ any one of Powhatan's daughters could have been the Pocahontas of legend
   ◯ Pocahontas fell in love with John Smith and saved his life

35. Look at the expression arose from in paragraph 1. This expression is closest in meaning to
   ◯ developed from
   ◯ went up with
   ◯ was told during
   ◯ climbed to

36. What is true about the name Pocahontas, according to the passage?
   ◯ It was the real name of the girl nicknamed Matoaka.
   ◯ It meant that someone was playful.
   ◯ Only one girl was known to have used this name.
   ◯ Powhatan was one of several people to be given this nickname.

37. Click on the sentence in paragraph 2 that indicates how Pocahontas was treated when she was under arrest at Jamestown.

38. It can be inferred from the passage that Pocahontas
    - ○ never intended to return to Virginia
    - ○ had a long marriage
    - ○ suffered from a long illness
    - ○ did not mean to remain in England

39. Look at the word indeed in paragraph 3. This word is closest in meaning to
    - ○ therefore
    - ○ in fact
    - ○ unexpectedly
    - ○ in contrast

40. Click on the word in paragraph 3 that is closest in meaning to "personally familiar."

41. Look at the word he in paragraph 3. Click on the word or phrase in paragraph 3 that he refers to.

42. Why are some historians doubtful about the portion of the Pocahontas folktale dealing with John Smith?
    - ○ Captain John Smith probably never knew Pocahontas.
    - ○ Captain John Smith was never actually in Jamestown.
    - ○ His rescue purportedly happened while Pocahontas was in England.
    - ○ His account of the rescue did not appear until well after the event supposedly happened.

43. Click on the word in paragraph 3 that is closest in meaning to "truth."

44. The following sentence could be added to paragraph 3.

    However, other historians do argue quite persuasively that this incident did truly take place.

    Where would it best fit in the paragraph? Click on the square (■) to add the sentence to the paragraph.

Turn to page 178, and circle the numbers of the questions that you missed.

THE WRITING SECTION

The Writing section appears on the TOEFL® Computer-Based Test each time it is given, and the score from the Writing section counts as part of the score of the Structure section. The Writing section will be given at the end of the TOEFL® Computer-Based Test, after the Listening, Structure, and Reading sections.

In the Writing section, you will be given a specific question, and you will be asked to answer that question in essay format in 30 minutes. You may choose to write your essay on paper or to type your essay on the computer.

Because you must write a complete essay in such a short period of time, it is best for you to aim to write a basic, clear, concise, and well-organized essay. The following strategies should help you to write this type of essay.

STRATEGIES FOR THE WRITING SECTION

1. **Type your answer on the computer only if you are comfortable working on a computer.** You may choose to write your answer on paper if you are not comfortable using a computer. If you write by hand, write neatly.

2. **Read the question carefully, and answer the question exactly as it is asked.** Take several minutes at the beginning of the test to be sure that you understand the question and to outline a response to it.

3. **Organize your response very clearly.** You should think of having an introduction, body paragraphs that develop the introduction, and a conclusion to end your essay. Use transitions to help the reader understand the organization of ideas.

4. **Whenever you make any general statement, be sure to support that statement.** You can use examples, reasons, facts, or personal details to support any general statement.

5. **Stick to vocabulary, sentence structures, and grammatical points that you know.** This is not the time to try out new words or structures.

6. **Finish writing your essay a few minutes early so that you have time to edit what you wrote.** You should spend the last three to five minutes checking your essay for errors.

THE SCORE

The Writing section is graded on a scale of 0 to 6, and this score is included on your score report sheet. The score on the Writing section also counts as half of the scaled score in the Structure section of the TOEFL® Computer-Based Test. The following table outlines what each of the scores essentially means:

	THE WRITING SECTION
6.	The writer has very strong organizational, structural, and grammatical skills.
5.	The writer has good organizational, structural, and grammatical skills. However, the essay contains some errors.
4.	The writer has adequate organizational, structural, and grammatical skills. The essay contains a number of errors.
3.	The writer shows evidence of organizational, structural, and grammatical skills that still need to be improved.
2.	The writer shows a minimal ability to convey ideas in written English.
1.	The writer is not capable of conveying ideas in written English.
0.	The paper is blank or contains nothing more than the topic.

SAMPLE ESSAYS

This section contains six essays, one demonstrating each of the six possible scores. These essays can give you some idea of the type of essay you need to write to achieve a good score. They can also demonstrate some of the major errors you should avoid in the Writing section.

   The strengths and weaknesses of each essay have been outlined at the end of each. It would be helpful to study each answer in order to understand what is good and what is not so good in each of these essays.

   This is the topic that was used:

Writing

Sample Essay Topic
Time — 30 minutes

Do you agree or disagree with the following statement?

Some people place a high value on loyalty to the employer. To others, it is perfectly acceptable to change jobs every few years to build a career. Discuss these two positions. Then indicate which position you agree with and why.

Use specific reasons and details to support your answer.

The following essay received a score of 6:

Different cultures place varying values on loyalty to the employer. In some countries, most notably in Asia, there is a high degree of loyalty to one company. However, in most European countries and the United States, loyalty to one's employer is not highly valued; instead it is considered more rationel and reasonable for an employee to change jobs whenever it is waranted to achieve the optimal overall career. Both of these positions have advantages and disadvantages.

In cultures that value loyalty to the employer, a kind of family relationship seems to develop between employer and employee. It is a reciprocal arrangement which the employer is concerned with asisting the employee to develop to his/her full potential and the employee is concerned about optimizing the welfare of the company. The negative aspect to absolute loyalty to one company is that an employee may stay in one job that he/she has outgrow and may miss out on opportunities to develop in new directions. From the employer's point of view, the employee may be burdened with employees whose skills no longer match the needs of the company.

In cultures in which it is quite acceptable to change jobs every few years, employees can build the career they choose for themself. They can stay with one company as long as it is mutually beneficial to company and employee. As long as good relationship exists and the employee's career is advancing at an acceptable pace, the employee can rmain with a company. But at any time the employee is free to move to another company, perhaps to achieve a higher position, to move into a new area, or to find a work situation that is more suitable to his/her personality. The disadvantage of this situation is employees tend to move around a lot.

Although both these systems have advantages and disadvantages, it is much better for employees have the opportunity to move from job to job if it is necessary to have a better career.

THE "6" ESSAY

Strengths of This Essay
1. It discusses all aspects of the topic.
2. It is clearly organized.
3. The ideas are well developed.
4. It has good, correct sentence structure.
5. It has only a few spelling and grammar errors.

Weaknesses of This Essay
1. The concluding paragraph is rather weak.

The following essay received a score of 5:

Some people place high value on loyalty to employer. They believe the company is responsible for the employee's career. The company will make decisions for the employee about his job. The company will decide to raise employee to new position or keep him in the old position. In this way the company will have overall plan for the good of the company and everyone in the company.

Other people believe it is perfectly acceptable to change jobs every few years to build a career. They believe employee is responsible for his own career. The employee will make decisions about his career. Employee will decide when to move to other company. Employee will choose what is good for employee rather than the company.

The best system is one when employer takes responsibility for the careers of employees. Employer should take responsibility. It is his duty. Employee knows that employer is watching out for his career. Then employee will work hard and do good job. He will be loyal to the company. This system works out best for everyone. It is best for both the company and employees.

THE "5" ESSAY

Strengths of This Essay
1. It discusses the topic fully.
2. It is clearly organized.
3. It has correct sentence structure.

Weaknesses of This Essay
1. The sentence structure is very simple.
2. There are some grammatical errors, particularly with articles.

The following essay received a score of 4:

Every one is not in agreement about how loyal people should be to their employers. Some people place a high value on loyalty to the employer. These people believe that they should work hard for their employer and so their employer will take care of them. To others it is perfectly acceptable to change jobs every few years to build a career. They believe that having only one employer and one job in a career will not be the best for them.

In my culture people stay with one employer for their whole life. They have a job they will work their hardest at that job because it is the only job they will have. They do not look for another job they already have one because that would be unloyal. This way is better because when you old the company will take care you and your family.

THE "4" ESSAY

Strengths of This Essay
1. It answers the question fairly well.
2. It is clearly organized.

Weaknesses of This Essay
1. It copies too directly from the question.
2. The ideas are not very well developed.
3. There are several examples of incorrect sentence structure.

The following essay received a score of 3:

Some people stay with one employeer for their entire career, but anothers build a career by changing jobs every few years. There are three reasens people should staying with on employer for their entire career.

First, the people should staying with one employer because it is best for the workers. If workers stay with one employer they will not having to move and they can learning all abou the company and advence in the company.

Second, people should staying with one employer because it is best for the compeny. The people will knowing how to do their jobs and they will having a big producton and the compeny will be very success.

Finally, people should staying with one employer because it is best for soceity. If people stay with one compeny then all the compenies will being very success. If all the compenie are very success then soceity will be success.

THE "3" ESSAY

Strengths of This Essay
1. It is clearly organized.
2. It has good, correct sentence structure.

Weaknesses of This Essay
1. It does not discuss the topic completely.
2. There are errors in spelling and grammar.

The following essay received a score of 2:

First, there is a disadvantage to place a high value on loyalty to the employer if your employer is no a good employer and your job is no a good job then you should no be loyal to a bad employer. Many employer are no good employers and if you are loyal to a bad employer it is a waste because a bad employer he will no be good to you.

Next, there is a advantage to change jobs every few years to build a carere if you get boring with your job and you want to move from one job to other so yo can get a better job instead of stay in your old boring job.

Finally, people should decide for themself where they want to work, if they decide one plce when they very young, how can they be sure whe they are older that they will still want to work there?

THE "2" ESSAY

Strengths of This Essay
1. The overall organization is clear.
2. The writer's main point is clear.

Weaknesses of This Essay
1. The sentence structure is poor.
2. There are numerous errors in spelling and grammar.
3. The ideas are not very well developed.

The following essay received a score of 1:

I think people should staying only one job for his hole careere. Because it is importent loyal to your jop. If you not loyal. Th company didn't be able has good business. If the employees keep change. New employees alway needs be train, and so on.

THE "1" ESSAY

Weaknesses of This Essay
1. It does not discuss the topic completely.
2. The ideas are disorganized and difficult to follow.
3. There are many errors in spelling and grammar.
4. There are many errors in sentence structure.
5. It is too short.

BEFORE WRITING

Skill 1: DECODING THE TOPIC

The first and most important step in the Writing section is to decode the topic to determine what the intended outline is. Writing topics generally give very clear clues about how your answer should be constructed. It is important to follow the clear clues that are given in the topic when you are planning your answer. You probably will not be given much credit for a response that does not cover the topic in the way that is intended. Study the following essay topic:

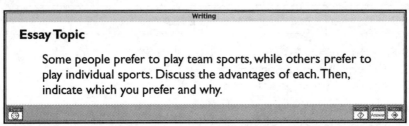

As you read this topic, you should think about the organization of the intended response that will be expected by test graders. Your essay should start with an introduction, and that introduction should mention *team sports, individual sports,* and their *advantages*. This introduction should be followed by supporting paragraphs describing the *advantages of team sports* and the *advantages of individual sports*. In the final paragraph, you should discuss whether *you prefer team* or *individual sports* and *why*. This final paragraph serves as your conclusion because it brings together the ideas in the previous paragraphs about team and individual sports. The following is an appropriate outline for an essay on the topic above:

Paragraph 1:	INTRODUCTORY PARAGRAPH *(mentioning the advantages of team and individual sports)*
Paragraph 2:	FIRST SUPPORTING PARAGRAPH *(listing and discussing the advantages of team sports)*
Paragraph 3:	SECOND SUPPORTING PARAGRAPH *(listing and discussing the advantages of individual sports)*
Paragraph 4:	CONCLUDING PARAGRAPH *(whether you prefer team or individual sports and why)*

The following chart outlines the key information that you should remember about decoding writing topics:

DECODING THE WRITING TOPIC
Each topic in the Writing section shows you exactly *what* you should discuss and *how* you should organize your response. You must decode the topic carefully to determine the intended way of organizing your response.

EXERCISE 1: For each of the following writing topics, indicate the type of information that you will include in each paragraph of your response.

> 1. What do you think is the best age to marry? Give reasons and examples for your opinion.

INTRODUCTION: *the best age to marry*
SUPPORTING PARAGRAPH 1: *first reason why this is the best age (with examples)*
SUPPORTING PARAGRAPH 2: *second reason why this is the best age (with examples)*
SUPPORTING PARAGRAPH 3: *third reason why this is the best age (with examples)*
CONCLUSION: *summary of best age for marriage and reasons why*

> 2. Do you agree or disagree with the following statement?
>   *Actions speak louder than words.*
>   Use specific reasons and examples to support your opinion.

> 3. Some people work more effectively during the day, while other people work much more effectively at night. Discuss which type of person you are. Give reasons and examples to support your response.

> 4. What historical event in your country has had a major effect on your country? Give reasons and examples to support your response.

5. Some people prefer to take a position in a company and work for the company. Other people think it is much better to go into business for themselves. Which do you think is better? Give reasons and examples to support your response.

6. It can be quite difficult to learn a new language. What do you think are the most difficult aspects of learning a new language? Give reasons and examples to support your response.

7. Do you agree or disagree with the following statement?

    I think there is too much violence in movies.

    Use specific reasons and examples to support your opinion.

8. Some people think that it is a good idea to explore the universe around us, while others think it is a good idea to explore the unknown areas of our own world. Still others think that it is best to work to improve the known parts of the planet rather than spending so much to explore unknown areas. Which position do you agree with most? Give reasons and examples to support your opinion.

Skill 2: DEVELOPING SUPPORTING IDEAS

After you have decoded a writing topic to determine the overall organization of your response, you need to plan how to develop your ideas. You need to provide as much support as possible for the ideas in your essay, using reasons and examples and making your answer as personal as possible. To have an effective essay, you need strong support.

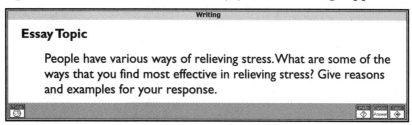

Essay Topic

People have various ways of relieving stress. What are some of the ways that you find most effective in relieving stress? Give reasons and examples for your response.

As you read this topic, you should quickly determine that the overall organization of your response should be an introduction, supporting paragraphs about your ways of relieving stress (with examples of and reasons for your choices), and a conclusion. You should take a few minutes before you begin writing to develop your ideas.

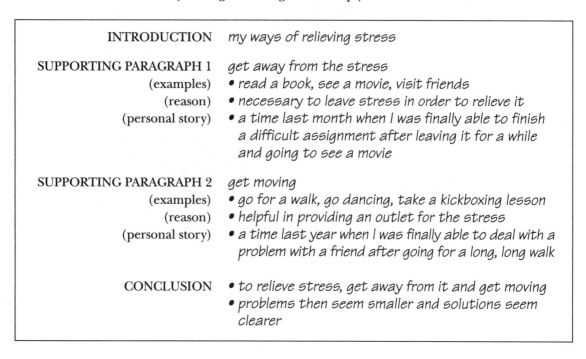

INTRODUCTION	*my ways of relieving stress*
SUPPORTING PARAGRAPH 1	*get away from the stress*
(examples)	• *read a book, see a movie, visit friends*
(reason)	• *necessary to leave stress in order to relieve it*
(personal story)	• *a time last month when I was finally able to finish a difficult assignment after leaving it for a while and going to see a movie*
SUPPORTING PARAGRAPH 2	*get moving*
(examples)	• *go for a walk, go dancing, take a kickboxing lesson*
(reason)	• *helpful in providing an outlet for the stress*
(personal story)	• *a time last year when I was finally able to deal with a problem with a friend after going for a long, long walk*
CONCLUSION	• *to relieve stress, get away from it and get moving*
	• *problems then seem smaller and solutions seem clearer*

In this example, there are two main ideas for handling stress: *get away from the stress* and *get moving*. Each of these ideas is supported by examples, a reason, and personal information.

The following chart outlines the key information that you should remember about the development of supporting ideas:

DEVELOPING SUPPORTING IDEAS

Support your essay with *reasons* and *examples*, and *personalize* your essay as much as possible. The more support you have, the stronger your essay will be.

EXERCISE 2: For each of the following topics, develop ideas to support it using reasons, examples, and personal information.

> 1.   What famous place would you like to visit? Use specific reasons and examples to support your choice.

> 2.   Compare yourself today and yourself five years ago. In what ways are you the same or different? Use specific examples to support your response.

> 3.   What recent news story has affected you the most? In what ways has it affected you? Use specific reasons and examples to support your response.

> 4.   Some people prefer to work in one company for all their career. Others think it is better to move from company to company to build a career. Discuss the advantages of each position. Which do you think is better, and why?

5. Many families have important traditions that family members share. What is one of your family's important traditions? Use specific reasons and examples to support your response.

6. Traveling in a different country and different culture can be exciting but can also be frustrating. What are the most important pieces of advice that you would give to visitors coming to your country? Use specific reasons and examples to support your response.

7. Do you agree or disagree with the following statement?
      Haste makes waste.
   Use specific reasons and examples to support your opinion.

8. Some people show their emotions, while other people work hard to keep their emotions from showing. What are the advantages of each type of behavior? Which do you try to do?

WHILE WRITING

Skill 3: WRITING THE INTRODUCTORY PARAGRAPH

The purpose of the introduction is first to interest the reader in your topic and then to explain clearly to the reader what you are going to discuss. When finished with your introduction, the reader should be eager to continue on with your essay, and the reader should have an exact idea of your topic and how you are going to organize the discussion of your topic. You do not need to give the outcome of your discussion in the introduction; you can save that for the conclusion.

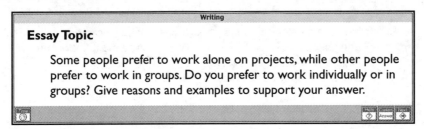

> **Writing**
>
> **Essay Topic**
>
> Some people prefer to work alone on projects, while other people prefer to work in groups. Do you prefer to work individually or in groups? Give reasons and examples to support your answer.

The following example shows one possible introduction to an essay on this topic.

INTRODUCTION 1

In my job as an engineer, I have worked on numerous projects, some of which have been individual projects and others of which have been group projects. Each time I worked individually on a project, I seemed to wish that I had a group to work with, and each time I worked in a group I seemed to wish that I could finish the project myself. Each type of work style has its own advantages.

The first part of this introduction gives background information about the writer to interest the reader in the essay. The first two sentences tell the reader that the writer works as an engineer and has had experience working both individually and in groups on engineering projects. The last sentence of the introduction tells the reader how the essay will be developed. From the last sentence of the introduction, it can be determined that the writer will discuss the advantages of one style of work and then the advantages of the other style of work.

The next example shows a different way that an essay on the topic above could be introduced.

INTRODUCTION 2

The educational system where I have been a student for the last sixteen years is a system that places a high value on individual achievement and little value on group achievement. Having been a rather successful student in this educational system for the better part of my life, I am well aware of the advantages of working individually on projects. However, I can only imagine the advantages of working on projects in groups.

The first part of this introduction informs the reader that the writer has been a successful student in an educational system that is based on a lot of individual work. By the end of the introduction, the reader understands that the writer intends to discuss the advantages of individual work, based on personal experience, and the advantages of working in groups, from her or his imagination.

The following chart outlines the key information that you should remember about writing introductory paragraphs:

WRITING THE INTRODUCTORY PARAGRAPH

1. Begin the introduction with *background* information about how the topic relates to you in order to get the reader *interested* in your essay.
2. End the introduction with a statement or statements that show the reader how the rest of the essay will be *organized*.

EXERCISE 3: Write introductory paragraphs for essays on the following topics. In each introductory paragraph, circle the *background* information that shows how the topic relates to you. Underline the information that shows how the rest of the essay will be *organized*.

1. Which movie that you have seen has affected you the most? Use specific reasons and examples to support your answer.

2. Various types of people achieve success in life. What do you think are the most important characteristics necessary to achieve success? Use reasons and examples to support your ideas.

3. Do you agree or disagree with the following statement?
   People should always express their opinions.
   Use specific reasons and examples to support your answer.

4. If you could choose to meet any famous person (living or dead), which person would you choose? Use reasons and details to support your choice.

5. Some school systems require students to study a foreign language, while other school systems do not. Do you think that the study of a foreign language should be required? Use reasons and examples to support your ideas.

Skill 4: WRITING UNIFIED SUPPORTING PARAGRAPHS

A good way to write a clear and effective supporting paragraph is to begin with a sentence to introduce the main idea of the passage, support the main idea with strong details, and connect the ideas together in a unified paragraph. The following outline shows a paragraph topic and its supporting ideas.

---

benefits of television
- *provides an awareness of local and world news*
- *provides an awareness of other people's feelings*
- *provides an awareness of current trends, styles, slang*

Various methods can be used to connect ideas together in a unified paragraph: (1) repeating a key word, (2) rephrasing the key word, (3) referring to the key word with a pronoun or possessive, and (4) adding transition words or phrases. The paragraph based on the outline above contains examples of each of these methods of unifying the ideas in a paragraph.

Although much has been said about the evils of watching too much television, I would like to make a case in support of the benefits of television. In a variety of ways, television helps to keep you aware of the world around you. The first way that this modern mechanical marvel increases your awareness is through news programs. Through them, you become at least somewhat acquainted with happenings from around the world and in your own back yard. Television keeps you aware not just of the facts from news programs but also of opinions. Through talk shows and discussion programs, it helps you to be familiar with how other members of society feel about issues.

A final way that television helps to keep you aware of your surroundings is to show you the current trends, styles, and slang that are common in today's world. By watching television programs, you can keep up with what people are doing, what they are wearing, and what they are saying.

This paragraph contains numerous examples of devices that make the paragraph more unified. (1) The key word *television* is repeated various times, rephrased as *this modern mechanical device,* and replaced with the pronoun *it.* (2) The key word *program* is repeated several times, rephrased as *shows,* and referred to with the pronoun *them.* (3) The key word *aware* is repeated several times and rephrased as *acquainted, familiar,* and *keep up.* (4) The transition phrases *the first way* and *the final way* are used to introduce the first benefit of television *(awareness of...news)* and the third benefit of television *(awareness of current trends...).* (5) The transition sentence *television keeps you aware not just of the facts from news programs but also of opinions* relates the first benefit of television *(awareness of...news)* and the second benefit of television *(awareness of other people's feelings).*

The following chart outlines the key information that you should remember when you are writing supporting paragraphs:

WRITING UNIFIED SUPPORTING PARAGRAPHS
Introduce each supporting paragraph with a *topic sentence* and support that paragraph with lots of *details.* Make sure that the ideas in the paragraph are unified by using a mixture of the following methods: • repeating a key word • rephrasing a key word • replacing a key word with a pronoun • adding transition expressions • adding transition sentences
NOTE: See 7B on page 136 for examples of transition expressions.

EXERCISE 4: Read the paragraph. Then, follow these directions:

1. Find the word *difficult* in the passage. How many times is it repeated?
2. Find the word *problem(s)* in the passage. How many times is it repeated?
3. Find a transition expression showing that an *example* will follow.
4. Find a transition sentence between the two examples.
5. Find the noun that the pronoun *it* (line 4) refers to.
6. Find the noun that the pronoun *it* (line 13) refers to.
7. Find one way that *strange response* (line 5) is rephrased.
8. Find three ways that *Dunno* (line 6) is rephrased.
9. Find one way that *surprised* (line 8) is rephrased.

English is not an easy language to learn. Of all the possible problems that I have experienced when trying to learn this language, the most difficult problem that I have encountered is that English does not seem to be spoken by

Line Americans in the same way that it was presented in my textbooks. For instance,
(5) the first time that I asked an American a question, I got a strange response. The man who answered my question said something that sounded like "Dunno." I was sure that I had never studied this expression in my textbooks, and I could not find anything like it in my dictionary. I was surprised to learn later from a friend that this mysterious-sounding phrase was really nothing more than a
(10) shortened version of "I do not know." Not too long after that I had an even more interesting example of my most difficult problem in learning English. One evening, I was unable to do a chemistry homework assignment, so the next morning I asked a classmate if she had been able to do it. I was amazed when she gave the rather bizarre answer that the assignment had been a "piece of cake." I was not
(15) quite sure what a "piece of cake" had to do with the chemistry assignment, so I responded that I was not sure that the assignment really was a piece of cake. I have by now learned that she meant that the assignment was quite easy. You can see from these two examples what I find so difficult about the English language.

Now, write a paragraph beginning with *The most (interesting / exciting / embarrassing / frightening) day in my life occurred....* Then, follow these directions:

1. Circle each key word the first time that it appears in the paragraph. Draw a line from the key word to any repetitions, rephrases, or pronoun references to that key word.
2. Underline any transition phrases once.
3. Underline any transition sentences twice.

Skill 5: WRITING THE CONCLUDING PARAGRAPH

The purpose of the conclusion is to close your essay by summarizing the main points of your discussion. When finished with your conclusion, the reader should clearly understand your exact ideas on the topic and the reasons you feel the way that you do about the topic.

The ideas in your conclusion should be clearly related to the ideas that you began in the introduction. While in the introduction you should indicate what you intend to discuss in the essay, in the conclusion you should indicate the outcome or results of the discussion. Refer to the essay topic and sample introductions in Skill 3.

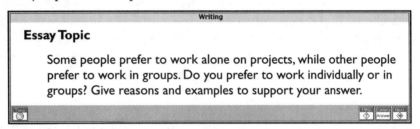

Essay Topic

Some people prefer to work alone on projects, while other people prefer to work in groups. Do you prefer to work individually or in groups? Give reasons and examples to support your answer.

The following paragraph is a conclusion to the essay that began with INTRODUC-TION 1 (in Skill 3).

> CONCLUSION 1
>
> *Even though it can be nice to work alone because I can use the pace, methods, and criteria that I like, I actually prefer working in groups. It is necessary to put up with a bit of frustration in group projects, but there is a worthwhile trade-off. The interactions with others, the open exchanges of ideas, and the opportunity to learn from others and to share with others make group projects more rewarding to me in the long run.*

In this conclusion, the writer summarizes the advantages of each style of work: working individually is better because a person can decide on the *pace, methods, and criteria,* while working in groups is better because of *the interactions with others, the open exchanges of ideas, and the opportunity to learn from others and to share with others.* The writer also clearly states the opinion that working in groups is preferable.

The next paragraph is a conclusion to the essay that began with INTRODUCTION 2 (in Skill 3).

> CONCLUSION 2
>
> *I have worked individually throughout my education, and I have been successful working in this way because this style of work is a good match with my personality. I can imagine that, for some people, the cooperative benefits that come from working in groups might be a good thing. However, I prefer to continue with a style of work that has made me successful up to now. I hope that the success that I have had up to now by working in this way will continue to make me successful in the future.*

Here the writer briefly summarizes the advantages of each style of work by mentioning that working individually is *a good match with my personality* and that working in groups has *cooperative benefits*. The writer also clearly states a preference for working individually because of the success that this style of work has brought *up to now* and perhaps will continue to bring *in the future.*

The following chart outlines the key information that you should remember about writing concluding paragraphs:

WRITING THE CONCLUDING PARAGRAPH

1. *Summarize* the key points in your discussion.
2. Be sure that your overall *idea* and *reasons* for the idea are very *clear*.

EXERCISE 5: Write concluding paragraphs for the essays that you introduced in Skill 3. In each concluding paragraph, circle your overall idea. Underline the key points of your discussion.

1. Which movie that you have seen has affected you the most? Use specific reasons and examples to support your answer.

2. Various types of people achieve success in life. What do you think are the most important characteristics necessary to achieve success? Use reasons and examples to support your ideas.

3. Do you agree or disagree with the following statement?
   People should always express their opinions.
   Use specific reasons and examples to support your answer.

4. If you could choose to meet any famous person (living or dead), which person would you choose? Use reasons and details to support your choice.

5. Some school systems require students to study a foreign language, while other school systems do not. Do you think that the study of a foreign language should be required? Use reasons and examples to support your ideas.

Skill 6: CONNECTING THE SUPPORTING PARAGRAPHS IN THE ESSAY

To make your essay as clear as possible, you should show as clearly as you can how the ideas in the supporting paragraphs in your essay are related. This can be accomplished (1) with transition expressions such as *the first, the most important,* or *a final way,* or (2) with transition sentences that include the idea of the previous paragraph and the idea of the current paragraph. It is best to use a combination of these two types of transitions. The following example shows how transitions can be used to show the relationships among the supporting paragraphs in an essay:

ESSAY OUTLINE	
(introduction)	*the qualities that I admire most in a boss*
(supporting paragraph 1)	*• patience*
(supporting paragraph 2)	*• organization*
(supporting paragraph 3)	*• fairness*
TRANSITIONS	
(to introduce SP1)	*One important quality that I find essential in a boss is patience.*
(to introduce SP2)	*In addition to a patient boss, I would like an organized boss.*
(to introduce SP3)	*A final quality that I look for in a boss is fairness.*

The first supporting paragraph is introduced with the transition expression *One important quality* to show that this is the first of the qualities that you are going to discuss in your essay. The second supporting paragraph is introduced with a transition sentence that shows how this paragraph is related to the previous paragraph; it includes a reference to the first supporting paragraph *a patient boss* and a reference to the second supporting paragraph *an organized boss.* The third supporting paragraph is introduced with the transition expression *A final quality* to show that this is the last of the three qualities that you admire in a boss.

The following chart outlines the important information to remember about connecting the supporting paragraphs of your essay:

CONNECTING THE SUPPORTING PARAGRAPHS OF THE ESSAY
1. The supporting paragraphs of an essay can be connected with *transition expressions* or with *transition sentences.*
2. It is best to use a *combination* of these two types of transitions.

EXERCISE 6: For each outline of an essay, write sentences to introduce each of the supporting paragraphs. You should use a combination of transition expressions and transition sentences.

1. **INTRO:**   *a decision about whether or not to own a car in a big city*
    SP1:   • the advantages of owning a car in a big city
    SP2:   • the disadvantages of owning a car in a big city

    SP1:   The advantages of having a car in a big city are numerous.

    SP2:   There may be numerous advantages to owning a car in a big city; however,
    there are also distinct disadvantages.

2. **INTRO:**   *the types of reading that I enjoy*
    SP1:   • science fiction
    SP2:   • romances
    SP3:   • sports magazines

    SP1:   _____

    SP2:   _____

    SP3:   _____

3. **INTRO:**   *a preference for traveling alone or traveling in groups*
    SP1:   • benefits of traveling alone
    SP2:   • benefits of traveling in groups

    SP1:   _____

    SP2:   _____

4. **INTRO:**   *characteristics leading to success as a student*
    SP1:   • self-motivation
    SP2:   • attention to detail
    SP3:   • desire to succeed
    SP4:   • joy of learning

    SP1:   _____

    SP2:   _____

    SP3:   _____

    SP4:   _____

5. INTRO: *living for today versus living for tomorrow*
    SP1: • people who have a philosophy of living for today
    SP2: • people who have a philosophy of living for tomorrow

    SP1: _____

    SP2: _____

6. INTRO: *my reasons for going to the movies*
    SP1: • to be entertained rather than to be taught
    SP2: • to feel good rather than feel depressed
    SP3: • to escape reality rather than be immersed in reality

    SP1: _____

    SP2: _____

    SP3: _____

7. INTRO: *advice to someone trying to learn a new language*
    SP1: • listen to videos, television programs, radio programs in the new language
    SP2: • talk with native speakers of the language every chance you get
    SP3: • read newspapers, magazines, books in the new language
    SP4: • find a pen pal and write to someone in the new language

    SP1: _____

    SP2: _____

    SP3: _____

    SP4: _____

8. INTRO: *steps the government should take to protect the earth's environment*
    SP1: • educate the population about the causes and effects of damage to the environment
    SP2: • create and enforce laws that penalize individuals and companies that damage the
      environment
    SP3: • reward environmentally conscious individuals and companies with tax incentives

    SP1: _____

    SP2: _____

    SP3: _____

AFTER WRITING

Skill 7: EDITING SENTENCE STRUCTURE

7A. Simple Sentence Structure

A *simple* sentence is a sentence that has only one **clause.**[1] Two types of sentence structure errors are possible in sentences with only one clause: (1) the clause can be missing a subject or a verb, and (2) the clause can be introduced by a subordinate clause connector.

The first type of incorrect simple sentence is a sentence that is missing a subject or a verb. (Note that an asterisk is used to indicate that the sentence contains an error.)

> Generally, <u>is</u> important to fill out the form completely.*
>   VERB

> The <u>ideas</u> for the construction of the project.*
>   SUBJECT

The first sentence is incorrect because it has the verb *is* but is missing a subject. The second sentence is incorrect because it has a subject *ideas* but is missing a verb.

A sentence structure with both a subject and a verb is not always correct. If the one clause in the sentence includes both a subject and a verb but is introduced by a subordinate clause connector, then the sentence is also incomplete.

> Because the <u>manager</u> of the company <u>instructed</u> me to do it.*
>   SUBJECT   VERB

> What the <u>rules</u> of the contest <u>indicated</u> about this situation.*
>   SUBJECT   VERB

The first sentence includes both a subject, *manager,* and a verb, *instructed,* but this sentence is not correct because it is introduced by the subordinate clause connector *Because.* The second sentence includes both a subject, *rules,* and a verb, *indicated,* but this sentence is not correct because it is introduced by the subordinate clause connector *What.*

The following chart outlines what you should remember about editing simple sentences:

EDITING SIMPLE SENTENCES
1. A simple sentence is a sentence with *one clause*.
2. A simple sentence must have both a *subject* and a *verb*.
3. A simple sentence may not be introduced by a *subordinate clause connector*.

---

[1]A **clause** is a group of words that has both a subject and a verb. Simple sentences with only one main clause are covered in great detail in Skills 1-5 of the Structure and Written Expression section of *Longman Preparation Course for the TOEFL® Test: Volume A, 2nd edition.*

EXERCISE 7A: Underline the subjects once and the verbs twice. Put boxes around the subordinate clause connectors. Then, indicate if the sentences are correct (C) or incorrect (I).

__I__   1.   The obvious <u>reasons</u> for the selection of the candidate.

_____   2.   Why everyone in the room did not believe the explanation.

_____   3.   I found his ideas rather unsettling.

_____   4.   Often discusses the advantages of the situation.

_____   5.   A preference for movies with lots of action and excitement.

_____   6.   Fortunately, the piece of paper with the crucial information was found.

_____   7.   How the article in the newspaper described the event.

_____   8.   Definitely is not proper to make that suggestion.

_____   9.   His agreement with me about the important issues.

_____   10. It happened that way.

_____   11. Because no one else in the world would have made the same decision.

_____   12. Without any hesitation made a decision not to return.

_____   13. An agreement as to the amount to be paid has been reached.

_____   14. A poem written on a piece of faded parchment.

_____   15. Just what you told me about your childhood.

_____   16. We forgot.

_____   17. To take the medicine at the right time to be the most effective.

_____   18. If you think about the problem just a little more.

_____   19. Unfortunately, the decision has already been made by the manager.

_____   20. Why you gave me a gift for my birthday.

7B. Compound Sentence Structure

A *compound* sentence is a sentence that has more than one **main clause.**[2] The main clauses in a compound sentence can be connected correctly with either a coordinate conjunction (*and, but, so, or, for, yet*) and a comma (see Skill 6 in Volume A) or with a semi-colon (*;*).

> Sally studies hard. She gets high grades.
> Sally studies hard, so she gets high grades.
> Sally studies hard; she gets high grades.

In the first example, the two main clauses *Sally studies hard* and *She gets high grades* are not connected into a compound sentence. In the second example, the two main clauses are combined into a compound sentence with the coordinate conjunction *so* and a comma. In the third example, the same two main clauses are combined into a compound sentence with a semi-colon.

It is possible to use adverb transitions in compound sentences. It is important to note that adverb transitions are not conjunctions, so either a coordinate conjunction with a comma or a semi-colon is needed.

> Sally studies hard. As a result, she gets high grades.
> Sally studies hard, and she gets high grades as a result.
> Sally studies hard; as a result, she gets high grades.

In the first example, the two main clauses *Sally studies hard* and *she gets high grades* are not combined into a compound sentence even though the adverb transition *As a result* is used. In the second example, the two main clauses are combined into a compound sentence with the coordinate conjunction *and* and a comma; the adverb transition *as a result* is included at the end of the compound sentence. In the third example, the same two main clauses are combined into a compound sentence with a semi-colon, and the adverb transition is set off from the second main clause with a comma.

The following chart lists some commonly used adverb transitions:

ADVERB TRANSITIONS			
TIME	CAUSE	CONTRAST	CONDITION
afterwards *next* *then* *finally*	*as a result* *consequently* *therefore*	*however* *in contrast*	*otherwise*

---

[2]**A main clause** is an independent clause that has both a subject and a verb. It is not introduced by a subordinate connector. Compound sentences are covered in Skill 6 of the Structure and Written Expression section of *Longman Preparation Course for the TOEFL® Test: Volume A, 2nd edition.*

EXERCISE 7B: Underline the subjects once and the verbs twice in the main clauses. Put boxes around the punctuation, transitions, and connectors that join the main clauses. Then, indicate if the sentences are correct (C) or incorrect (I).

_I_   1. The matter was really important, I could not decide too quickly.

_____   2. The children broke the rules, but their parents did not find out.

_____   3. She expected to graduate in the spring, however she did not graduate until fall.

_____   4. My family moved a lot during my youth; as a result, I always had to make new friends.

_____   5. I made a firm promise to my friend and I vowed to keep it.

_____   6. Sam did not sign in before work, so he signed in afterwards.

_____   7. The students waited in a long line to register. Finally, they got to the front of the line.

_____   8. His parents advised him to think about it some more he did not take their advice.

_____   9. My first job in the company was as a part-time worker, later I was given a full-time job.

_____   10. Tom really wanted to be successful, yet he did not know how to accomplish this.

_____   11. We must return the books to the library today, otherwise we will have to pay a fine.

_____   12. She always tries not to get too angry. However, she sometimes loses her temper.

_____   13. Therefore she has gotten a job, she can pay all her bills.

_____   14. She had the surgery recommended by her doctor; as a result, she is doing better now.

_____   15. They left the money in a savings account, it began to collect some interest.

_____   16. I wanted to get a high-paying job last summer; unfortunately, this was impossible.

_____   17. I will have to study harder, or I will not be able to get a scholarship.

_____   18. An accident happened at the corner; afterwards, the police came and wrote a report.

_____   19. The plan has a number of advantages it also has a number of disadvantages.

_____   20. The directions must be followed exactly, otherwise, the outcome will be very bad.

7C. Complex Sentence Structure

A *complex* sentence is a sentence that has at least one main clause and one **subordinate clause.**[3] Noun, adjective, and adverb clauses are all types of subordinate clauses. Each of these sentences is a complex sentence because it contains a subordinate clause:

I cannot believe (what he did).
NOUN CLAUSE

The runner (who finishes first) wins the trophy.
ADJECTIVE CLAUSE

I will return to the job (when I am able).
ADVERB CLAUSE

The first complex sentence contains the subordinate noun clause *what he did.* The second complex sentence contains the subordinate adjective clause *who finishes first.* The final complex sentence contains the subordinate adverb clause *when I am able.*

A variety of errors with complex sentence structures can occur in student writing, but the following two errors occur with great frequency: (1) repeated subjects after adjective clauses, and (2) repeated subjects after noun clauses as subjects.

A good friend (who lives down the street) she* did me a favor.
S   ADJECTIVE CLAUSE   S   V

(What my advisor told me) it* was very helpful.
NOUN CLAUSE - S   S   V

The first sentence is incorrect because it contains an extra subject. The correct subject *friend* comes before the adjective clause *who lives down the street,* and an extra subject *she* comes after the adjective clause. To correct this sentence, you should omit the extra subject *she.* The second sentence is also incorrect because it contains an extra subject. The noun clause *What my advisor told me* is a subject, and this noun clause subject is followed by an extra subject *it.* To correct this sentence, you should omit the extra subject *it.*

The following chart outlines what you should remember about editing complex sentences:

EDITING COMPLEX SENTENCES

1. When a subject comes before an adjective clause, do not add an extra subject after the adjective clause.
2. When a noun clause is used as a subject, do not add an extra subject after the noun clause.

---

[3]**A subordinate clause** is a dependent clause. It has both a subject and a verb and is introduced by a subordinate connector. Complex sentences with subordinate noun, adverb, and adjective clauses are covered in great detail in Skills 7-12 of the Structure and Written Expression section of *Longman Preparation Course for the TOEFL® Test: Volume A, 2nd edition.*

EXERCISE 7C: Underline the subjects once and the verbs twice in the main clauses. Put parentheses around the subordinate noun and adjective clauses. Then, indicate if the sentences are correct (C) or incorrect (I).

   I   1. The <u>reason</u> (that he took the money) <u>it</u> <u><u>was</u></u> to pay the bills.

   _____   2. Why that man did something so terrible will never be known.

   _____   3. The ticket that I needed to get onto the plane was not included in the packet.

   _____   4. What the lifeguard did it was quite heroic.

   _____   5. The day when I found out the news it was a good day.

   _____   6. The teacher whose advice I remember to this day was my sixth grade teacher.

   _____   7. Where we went on vacation it was such a gorgeous place.

   _____   8. That he really said those words it could not be refuted.

   _____   9. The man who helped me the most in my life he was my high school coach.

   _____   10. How the paper got finished on time remains unclear to me.

   _____   11. What caused the accident on the freeway it is still unknown.

   _____   12. The plans that we made for our trip were not very carefully thought out.

   _____   13. The process by which the decisions were made it was very slow.

   _____   14. Whatever she gets is what she deserves.

   _____   15. The employee who has the information that you need is out of the office today.

   _____   16. What he wrote in the letter it could not be taken back.

   _____   17. The officer who stopped me on the highway he gave me a ticket for speeding.

   _____   18. How he could believe something that is so incredible is beyond me.

   _____   19. The reason that I applied to the public school was that the tuition was lower.

   _____   20. Why they said what they said to the man who tried to help them it was not clear.

EXERCISE 7(A-C): Find and correct the sentence structure errors in the following essay. (The number in parentheses at the end of each paragraph indicates the number of errors in that paragraph.) The essay discusses the following topic.

> Do you agree or disagree with the following statement?
> *Taking part in sports helps prepare you for life.*
> Use specific reasons and details to explain your answer.

1.   I definitely believe that taking part in organized team sports is beneficial. However, is beneficial for much more than the obvious reasons. Everyone recognizes, of course, that participation in sports provides obvious physical benefits. It leading to improved physical fitness, it also provides a release from the stresses of life. I spent my youth taking part in a number of organized sports, including football, basketball, and volleyball, as a result of this experience I understand that the benefits of this participation go far beyond the physical benefits. (4 errors)

2.   One very valuable benefit that children get from taking part in team sports it is that it teaches participants teamwork. What any player in a team sport needs to learn it is that the individual team members must put the team ahead of individual achievement. Individuals on one team who are working for individual glory rather than the good of the team they often end up working against each other. A team made up of individuals unable to work together often not a very successful team. (4 errors)

3.   What also makes participation in team sports valuable it is that it teaches participants to work to achieve goals. Playing sports involves setting goals and working toward them, examples of such goals are running faster, kicking harder, throwing straighter, or jumping higher. Athletes learn that they can set goals and work toward them until the goals accomplished. Is through hard work that goals can be met. (4 errors)

4.   By taking part in sports, can learn the truly valuable skills of working together on teams and working to accomplish specific goals. These skills are not just beneficial in sports, more importantly the skills that are developed through sports they are the basis of success in many other aspects of life. Mastering these skills leading to success not only on the playing field but also in the wider arena of life. (4 errors)

Skill 8: EDITING WRITTEN EXPRESSION

8A. Inversions and Agreement

Errors in inversions and agreement are covered in the Structure and Written Expression section of *Longman Preparation Course for the TOEFL® Test, Volume A, 2nd edition.* You may want to review these skills.

>   **Skills 15-19: Inverted Subjects and Verbs**
>   **Skills 20-23: Problems with Subject/Verb Agreement**

EXERCISE 8A: Find and correct the errors in the following essay. (The number in parentheses at the end of each paragraph indicates the number of errors in that paragraph.) The essay discusses the following topic.

> What is something that you have tried once and that you will never try again? Use specific reasons and examples to support your response.

1.   Recently, some friends and I decided to try a camping trip to get a few days of much-needed relaxation. Only after we had begun this adventure we figured out what a mistake we had made. This experience in the woods have taught us that it is better to leave camping either to those who have experience or to those who have a higher degree of tolerance for the surprises of Mother Nature than does those of us on this trip. (3 errors)

2.   A few miles from our homes a lovely and serene campground is, and this seemed like a good place to begin our adventure. As we started out, the picturesque image that we had of camping trips were of cute little tents and roaring fires. Our first warning that our trip might not be what we had imagined came when did we try to put up our cute little tent. No sooner we had begun trying to get the tent up than we learned that this task was not going to be easy. We did finally get the tent up but were unsure of how long would it stay up. Then, when trying to build a fire, we discovered that our skill in building fires were no better than our skill in raising tents. After a lot more effort, none of the wood were burning, so we finally gave up. (7 errors)

3.   Even though we had problems because of our inexperience at camping, we still could have had a reasonable trip had not Mother Nature played a few surprises on us. Barely the sun had gone down when it started to rain. Feeling rather cold and wet as we huddled in our tent, we started wrapping sleeping bags around ourselves. Suddenly, there was several loud shrieks as a snake slithered out of one of the bags. At that point, each one of us were completely ready to end our camping adventure. An hour later, when were we checking into a motel, we had clearly arrived at the conclusion that camping was not for us. If were we to have the opportunity to go camping again, we would in all probability refuse instantly. (6 errors)

8B. Parallel, Comparative, and Superlative Structures

Errors in parallel, comparative, and superlative structures are covered in the Structure and Written Expression section of *Longman Student CD-ROM*. You may want to review these skills.

> **Skills 24-26: Problems with Parallel Structure**
> **Skills 27-29: Problems with Comparatives and Superlatives**

EXERCISE 8B: Find and correct the errors in the following essay. (The number in parentheses at the end of each paragraph indicates the number of errors in that paragraph.) The essay discusses the following topic.

> If you could start your own business, what would it be?
> Use specific reasons and examples to explain your answer.

1.   I am still a student, and I have neither started a business or even worked in someone else's company. However, one day when I am more old and more experienced, it is my dream to have my own business. If I could choose any business to start, I could not choose a most satisfying business than a travel agency. A travel agency would allow me not only to share the wonders of my country with others but also provide me with the opportunity to become familiar with the pleasantest places in the rest of the world. (5 errors)

2.   My country is beautiful, appeal, and unique. As a travel agent in my country, it would be my responsibility to familiarize visitors to my country with best that my culture has to offer. This is a responsibility that I would take part in with great pleasure. I would enjoy planning exciting tours for specific interests, such as local cuisine, crafts, or architectural. I would also offer extended travel packages for visitors who are more interested in relaxing and enjoy the beauty of my country then in rushing around. (5 errors)

3.   Another advantage of owning a travel agency is that it would allow me to become most knowledgeable about other places in the world than I currently am. The more educated I am about other places, I would be more able to assist in planning trips outside of my country. I would also have the opportunity as a travel agent to take trips myself and seeing exciting places with my own eyes. I have read extensively about many places in the world, studied art from many places in the world, and to see movies made in other places in the world. I would love to visit the places that I so far know only in books, in studies, and movies. It would be my responsibility as a travel agent to learn everything I could about other places, and this, too, seems like the wonderfulest responsibility. (6 errors)

4.   A travel agency probably would make me neither the richest nor more famous man in the world, but it still seems like an enjoyable and enrich company to own. Owning a company that requires me to learn all I can about most exciting places of all within my own country and in other countries of the world would be the more satisfying to me than own any other type of company. (5 errors)

8C. Verbs

Errors in verbs are covered in the Structure and Written Expression section of *Longman Student CD-ROM*. You may want to review these skills.

Skills 30-32: Problems with the Form of the Verb
Skills 33-36: Problems with the Use of the Verb
Skills 37-38: Problems with Passive Verbs

EXERCISE 8C: Find and correct the errors in the following essay. (The number in parentheses at the end of each paragraph indicates the number of errors in that paragraph.) The essay discusses the following topic.

> What is the most unexpected event that has happened in your life? Use specific reasons and examples to support your choice.

1.   The most unexpected event in my life occurs on my wedding day, when I was left standing alone at the altar. Prior to this rather memorable day, I have fallen in love with a wonderful woman and had ask her to become my wife. When she agreed, I thought that I will be the happiest man in the world. (4 errors)

2.   On the day of our wedding, however, a big surprise was wait for me. This wonderful fiancée of mine did not show up at the church for the 2:00 ceremony. During that long afternoon, the guests and I have waited, patiently at first and then quite impatiently. After more than an hour, I was convince that she had not show up because she has decided not to marry me. (5 errors)

3.   I am feeling quite devastated, almost suicidal, when suddenly a taxicab pulled up and my bride and her three bridesmaids dropped off in front of the church in rather dirtied gowns. Their car had broke down in a deserted area on the way to the church, and they had had to hike for a while until a cab could be find. After I recover from my shock, the wedding took place. (5 errors)

4.   Even though the shock of standing alone at the altar is quite hard for me, I learned a valuable lesson from this experience. I found out just how sad I will be to lose this woman, and I become even more thankful since that day to have her with me. (3 errors)

8D. Nouns and Pronouns

Errors in nouns and pronouns are covered in the Structure and Written Expression section of *Longman Student CD-ROM*. You may want to review these skills.

Skills 39-42: Problems with Nouns
Skills 43-45: Problems with Pronouns

EXERCISE 8D: Find and correct the errors in the following essay. (The number in parentheses at the end of each paragraph indicates the number of errors in that paragraph.) The essay discusses the following topic.

> What has been humanity's greatest technological achievement up to now? Use specific reasons and examples to support your choice.

1.   Humanity has accomplished so much great things that it is quite difficult to select one single technological achievements as humanity's greatest. To I, humanity's greatest achiever up to now has been the landing on the moon. It represents an extraordinary mixture of successful advanced technologist and the emotional payback that comes from succeeding at something fantastic. (5 errors)

2.   The amount of technological requirements for sending a manned spacecraft to the moon, having them successfully land on the lunar surface, and allowing humans to climb out of the spacecraft to explore theirs new surroundings was huge. It took a tremendous amount of effort of much people working together for incredibly long periods of time under a huge amount of pressure with few space for error. A single tiny miscalculation could lead to a crises. (6 errors)

3.   Even more important than the technological successor of the moon landing was the perspective of our home from the moon that this event provided us. This view of the earth from the moon provided every ones of we humans back on Earth with a whole new vision of our planet and their place in the universe. From our position on Earth, it often seems that us are at the center of the universe (in spite of how those diagrams in science texts portrayed our solar system and it's place in the universe). From the moon, though, we could clearly see the earth in a whole new way. This venture was the stimuli for developing an entirely different view of our planet. (7 errors)

8E. Adjectives and Adverbs

Errors in adjectives and adverbs are covered in the Structure and Written Expression section of *Longman Student CD-ROM.* You may want to review these skills.

Skills 46-48: Problems with Adjectives and Adverbs
Skills 49-51: More Problems with Adjectives
Skills 52-55: Problems with Articles

EXERCISE 8E: Find and correct the errors in the following essay. (The number in parentheses at the end of each paragraph indicates the number of errors in that paragraph.) The essay discusses the following topic.

> Some people prefer to live in large cities, while others prefer to live in small towns. Which of these two life-styles do you prefer? Use specific reasons and examples to support your choice.

1. The question of whether it is preferably to live in a big city or a small town is one that I have thought about a lot. I have experienced both, I have a appreciation of what each type of life has to offer, and I have now developed a preference strong for one over the other. (3 errors)

2. Life in a big city has both benefits and drawbacks. There are always an exciting things to do in the city — places to visit, activities and events to enjoy. However, even though there is so much going on, the city can be overwhelmed with strangers who are continuous rushing around you and without anyone who will share all the city has to offer. Sometimes there are just so many people that you can get lost in crowd. In the city, you can feel lone in spite of the fact that you are surrounded by hundreds of thousands of people. (5 errors)

3. Country life sometimes seems so bored — day after day the same people do the same things. The life active in the far-off cities, as depicted on television, seems so much more attractively than the limited life that surrounds you. (3 errors)

4. I came from a small village rather than a large city. A village where I grew up seemed so dull, and I eager anticipated finishing high school and heading for an university in a big city. When I first arrived, the city impressed tremendously me. However, I learned quick that, because people in the city rushed around so much, they did not have a time for each other. People have more time to treat each other friendly in a small town, and that is the kind of life that I prefer. (7 errors)

8F. Prepositions and Usage

Errors in prepositions and usage are covered in the Structure and Written Expression section of *Longman Student CD-ROM.* You may want to review these skills.

Skills 56-57: Problems with Prepositions
Skills 58-60: Problems with Usage

EXERCISE 8F: Find and correct the errors in the following essay. (The number in parentheses at the end of each paragraph indicates the number of errors in that paragraph.) The essay discusses the following topic.

> There are similarities and differences between high school studies and university studies. What are the most outstanding similarities or differences between high school and university studies? Use specific reasons and examples to support your choice.

1.   On my first semester at the university, I was overwhelmed by how dislike university studies and high school studies were. In high school, I had easily been able to finish the amount of work that was assigned, and if at a certain occasion I did not complete an assignment, then the teacher quickly told me to make the work. The situation in the university was not at all alike the situation in high school. (5 errors)

2.   I was greatly surprised the volume of work assigned in the university. Alike high school courses which perhaps covered a chapter in two weeks, university courses regularly covered two or three chapters in one week and two or three another chapters the next week. In high school, I had been able to finish the assigned chapters, but in the university it was difficult for me to keep up all the chapters even though I did a huge effort. (5 errors)

3.   The role that the teacher took in motivating students to get work done was also very different in the university. In high school, if an assignment was unfinished at the date that it was due, my teacher would immediately let me know that I had done a mistake and needed to turn up the assignment immediately. In the university, however, professors did not check up my work to be sure that I was getting work done regularly. It was quite easy to put up studying in the beginning and really have to work hard later to try and catch up the others students. (7 errors)

4.   During my first year in the university, I had to do a decision to get things done by myself instead of relying in other to watch over me and ensure that I was doing all that I needed to. With so much more work, this was quite a difficult task to accomplish, but I now regularly try to make my best because I unlike falling so far behind. It seems that I have turned in a pretty motivated student. (6 errors)

Listening Scripts

The Short Dialogues, page 3
Example: SHORT DIALOGUES

(woman)	Did you hear the announcement about our flight?
(man)	I did, and I can't believe that the flight has been cancelled.
(woman)	Neither can I!
(narrator)	WHAT DOES THE WOMAN MEAN?

Diagnostic Pre-Test: SHORT DIALOGUES, page 5

1. *(woman)* That was some airshow.
   (man) It really was. The skydivers pulled off some incredible feats.
   (woman) I just couldn't believe what I saw!
   (narrator) WHAT DOES THE WOMAN MEAN?

2. *(man)* Can you tell me how I can find the biology lab from here?
   (woman) Just go down those steps, and enter the door after the first one.
   (narrator) WHAT SHOULD THE MAN DO?

3. *(woman)* Where are the dirty clothes? Have you taken care of them?
   (man) They're in the washing machine.
   (narrator) WHAT DOES THE MAN MEAN?

4. *(woman)* Let's look over the blueprints for the building one more time.
   (man) Good idea. We need to be sure that the design is absolutely correct before construction begins.
   (narrator) WHO ARE THESE PEOPLE MOST LIKELY TO BE?

5. *(man)* We got a letter today from the landlord.
   (woman) We did? What was in the letter?
   (man) It was not good news. The rent has been increased.
   (narrator) WHAT DOES THE MAN MEAN?

6. *(woman)* I just finished talking with Jack.
   (man) What did he have to say? Is he going with us to the restaurant tonight?
   (woman) I was unable to convince him to go.
   (narrator) WHAT DOES THE WOMAN MEAN?

7. *(woman)* How's the weather today?
   (man) It's just not as humid as it was last week.
   (narrator) WHAT DOES THE MAN SAY ABOUT THE WEATHER?

8. *(woman)* Can you believe that the department has changed the requirements for our major?
   (man) This change wasn't unexpected.
   (narrator) WHAT DOES THE MAN MEAN?

9. *(man)* Do you think that the restaurant was too expensive?
   (woman) I was surprised at the prices; we barely had enough to cover the bill!
   (narrator) WHAT DOES THE WOMAN MEAN?

10. *(man)* Did you enjoy the sightseeing trip that you took last week?
    (woman) It couldn't have been more perfect in any way.
    (narrator) WHAT DOES THE WOMAN MEAN?

11. *(woman)* We have another history exam on Friday.
    (man) I know. I hope this exam isn't as hard as the last one!
    (woman) You can say that again!
    (narrator) WHAT DOES THE WOMAN MEAN?

12. *(woman)* When do you think we should leave on our trip?
    (man) If we leave on Tuesday, we won't have very much time for a visit.
    (woman) Why not leave on Monday instead of Tuesday?
    (narrator) WHAT DOES THE WOMAN SUGGEST?

13. (woman)   I'll see you at the first psychology lecture tomorrow.
    (man)   Then you did enroll in the course!
    (narrator) WHAT HAD THE MAN ASSUMED?

14. (man)   I can't believe that there's going to be an exam tomorrow.
    (woman)   I wish the professor had announced the exam a little bit earlier.
    (narrator) WHAT DOES THE WOMAN IMPLY?

15. (woman)   Did our team win the game today?
    (man)   If the runner hadn't fallen, then our team would have won.
    (narrator) WHAT DOES THE MAN IMPLY?

16. (woman)   Where's the room for the conference?
    (man)   It's down the hall, on the right.
    (woman)   Is the room ready for the conference?
    (man)   I don't think it's been set up yet.
    (narrator) WHAT DOES THE MAN SAY ABOUT THE ROOM?

17. (man)   I'm not sure if we should try to buy a house in a few years or keep on renting.
    (woman)   We'll cross that bridge when we come to it!
    (narrator) WHAT DOES THE WOMAN MEAN?

Post-Test: SHORT DIALOGUES, page 9

1. (woman)   The results have been confirmed by several independent researchers.
    (man)   Then they must be accurate.
    (narrator) WHAT DOES THE MAN SAY ABOUT THE RESULTS?

2. (man)   I'm not ready to go out yet.
    (woman)   Do you know when you're going to be ready to leave?
    (man)   I hope we can go a bit later in the evening. I'd like to get a little rest before we go out.
    (narrator) WHAT DOES THE MAN WANT TO DO?

3. (woman)   Would you like to stop in here for a few minutes for a snack or a drink?
    (man)   That sounds like a good idea. I certainly am thirsty.
    (narrator) WHAT DOES THE MAN MEAN?

4. (man)   Can you tell me about any previous office experience you have?
    (woman)   I've worked as a receptionist in a doctor's office for a year and a half.
    (narrator) WHAT IS THE WOMAN PROBABLY DOING?

5. (man)   Has the lawyer received the letter yet?
    (woman)   The letter was delivered to the lawyer's office by courier just this morning.
    (narrator) WHAT DOES THE WOMAN MEAN?

6. (man)   Cathy's going to be able to come with us to the theater.
    (woman)   That's great! But doesn't she have to work tonight?
    (man)   Luckily, she was able to persuade her roommate to take her shift.
    (narrator) WHAT DOES THE MAN SAY ABOUT CATHY?

7. (woman)   What do you think of this accounting report?
    (man)   It doesn't seem to have been done very carefully.
    (narrator) WHAT DOES THE MAN IMPLY ABOUT THE REPORT?

8. (woman)   Is this year going to be easy or difficult for you?
    (man)   I'm going to work really hard this year and see if I can graduate in June.
    (woman)   It doesn't sound easy, but I don't think that's an unreachable goal.
    (narrator) WHAT DOES THE WOMAN THINK?

9. (woman)   Do you get to many of the university's football games?
    (man)   Only rarely.
    (narrator) WHAT DOES THE MAN MEAN?

10. (woman)   I was really surprised to see how Anna reacted.
    (man)   Did she accept the situation?
    (woman)   She couldn't have been more delighted!
    (narrator) HOW DID ANNA FEEL ABOUT THE SITUATION?

11. *(woman)*   That musical production was truly magnificent!
    (man)   I'll say!
    (narrator) WHAT DOES THE MAN MEAN?

12. *(man)*   It's an awfully long walk home, and I'm more than a little tired.
    (woman)   Let's take the bus instead of walking. Then you'll be able to get home quickly and get some sleep.
    (narrator) WHAT DOES THE WOMAN SUGGEST?

13. *(woman)*   Is Tom there? Could I talk with him please?
    (man)   Tom's not at home now. He's at work at the architectural firm.
    (woman)   Then he did get the job!
    (narrator) WHAT HAD THE WOMAN ASSUMED ABOUT TOM?

14. *(woman)*   Are you going to be taking microbiology this semester?
    (man)   I wish I could put off taking it for another semester, but I can't.
    (narrator) WHAT DOES THE MAN IMPLY?

15. *(man)*   Were you able to get a new computer?
    (woman)   If these computers hadn't gone on sale, then I just couldn't have afforded to buy one.
    (narrator) WHAT DOES THE WOMAN IMPLY?

16. *(man)*   Can I have an ashtray, please?
    (woman)   Oh, smoking isn't permitted here. You'll have to extinguish your cigarette.
    (narrator) WHAT DOES THE WOMAN ASK THE MAN TO DO WITH THE CIGARETTE?

17. *(woman)*   This assignment looks really long.
    (man)   And it looks really involved, too.
    (woman)   It does. Do you prefer to work on it alone or together?
    (man)   In this case, I think that two heads are better than one.
    (narrator) WHAT DOES THE MAN MEAN?

The Casual Conversations, page 13

Example: CASUAL CONVERSATIONS

(woman)   Look at this syllabus. It's really jam-packed.
(man)   It lists several chapters per week in the text that we have to get through. Each week, there are two chapters and sometimes three.
(woman)   And look. Sometimes, there are also supplementary readings in addition to the textbook chapters.
(man)   I don't know how I'm going to get through all this reading and prepare for the exams, too.
(woman)   My goodness, there are three unit exams spread throughout the course and then an overall final exam.
(man)   This course is going to take up an awful lot of my time.

(narrator) WHAT ARE THE WEEKLY READING ASSIGNMENTS LIKE IN THIS COURSE?
(narrator) HOW MANY TOTAL EXAMS ARE THERE IN THIS COURSE?

Exercise: CASUAL CONVERSATIONS, page 15

Questions 1-2

(woman)   You look lost. Can I help?
(man)   Oh, thanks. I hope so. I've been wandering around looking for Henderson Hall, and according to the map, it should be here, but I just can't find it.
(woman)   You're actually very close. Henderson Hall is just around the corner, on the other side of the building.
(man)   It is? I wonder how I could have missed it.
(woman)   You were probably just looking at the new, tall modern buildings. Henderson is actually just a small building and one of the oldest on campus. It's one of the original university buildings.
(man)   That must be why I missed it, then. Thanks so much for your help.
(woman)   You're quite welcome.

1. *(narrator)* WHAT PROBLEM DOES THE MAN HAVE?
2. *(narrator)* WHAT IS TRUE ABOUT HENDERSON HALL?

Questions 3-4

(man)	Did you hear about the study abroad program in the Art Department?
(woman)	I did, and it sounded really terrific!
(man)	A semester of study of Italian art here at the university and then a two-week trip to Italy during the semester break to see the art in person.
(woman)	I'm an art major, and Italian art is some of my favorite. I'd love to be able to take part.
(man)	I'm not an art major, but the whole thing sounds really wonderful to me.
(woman)	Unfortunately, it's something that I can't possibly afford, so I'll just have to dream about it.

3. *(narrator)*   WHAT IS INCLUDED IN THE STUDY ABROAD PROGRAM?
4. *(narrator)*   WHY ISN'T THE WOMAN TAKING PART IN THE STUDY ABROAD PROGRAM?

Questions 5-6

(woman)	I'm on my way to the Student Center. Would you like to come along?
(man)	What's going on there? I have a little time until my next class.
(woman)	I'm going to be meeting a couple of friends of mine for some coffee, and I can introduce you to them.
(man)	It would be nice to meet some new people, and I think I have time for one quick cup of coffee before class.
(woman)	How much time do you have? My next class isn't for an hour and a half.
(man)	I only have a half hour until my next class, so let's hurry on over.
(woman)	Sounds like a good idea to me!

5. *(narrator)*   WHEN IS THE WOMAN'S NEXT CLASS?
6. *(narrator)*   WHAT WILL THE STUDENTS PROBABLY DO NEXT?

Questions 7-9

(man)	Did you know that Dr. Benjamin is giving a talk tomorrow night in the University Theater?
(woman)	Who is Dr. Benjamin? Sorry, but I don't recognize the name.
(man)	Dr. Benjamin is the university's best known professor from the Environmental Studies Department, and he's giving another of his talks on environmental problems in the local areas surrounding the university.
(woman)	Another of his talks? Does he do this often?
(man)	He does. His talks are for the university community and the general public. The talks are always well attended because Dr. Benjamin is such a fascinating and knowledgeable lecturer.
(woman)	This talk tomorrow night sounds like something I shouldn't miss! I'll mark it on my calendar.

7. *(narrator)*   WHO IS DR. BENJAMIN?
8. *(narrator)*   WHAT IS MENTIONED ABOUT DR. BENJAMIN'S TALKS?
9. *(narrator)*   WHAT WILL THE WOMAN PROBABLY DO?

Questions 10-11

(woman)	So what did you think of the dance concert?
(man)	I thought it was pretty good, particularly considering that it was a school production and all the dancers in the program are students in the dance department. What about you?
(woman)	I thought the dancers were really well prepared and the performances went without any hitches, but it was just not the style of dance that I prefer.
(man)	Really? You don't like modern dance?
(woman)	Not so much, I guess. These dances were a little too modern for my taste. I like a more classical style of dance.
(man)	Then there's another concert, in two weeks, that you'll probably like a lot more.

10. *(narrator)*   WHAT WAS MENTIONED ABOUT THE DANCE PRODUCTION?
11. *(narrator)*   HOW DID THE WOMAN FEEL ABOUT THE PERFORMANCE?

Questions 12-14

(woman)	Would you like to play some tennis this afternoon, maybe around four o'clock?
(man)	Oh, I can't play tennis at four. I'll be at the library today from three to six o'clock. In fact, I go to the library every day from three o'clock to six o'clock.
(woman)	Do you always schedule every minute of every day? And then stick to the schedule?

(man)	Yes, every morning, one of the first things I do is to make a schedule for the day, and then I always try to follow the schedule as closely as possible.
(woman)	Well, my life certainly isn't as organized as yours, and I probably don't accomplish half as much as you. Maybe some other time for some tennis then, when you have time in your schedule.
(man)	That sounds like a great plan.

12. *(narrator)* WHY CAN'T THE MAN PLAY TENNIS TODAY?
13. *(narrator)* HOW MIGHT THE MAN'S LIFE BE DESCRIBED?
14. *(narrator)* WHAT DOES THE WOMAN SAY ABOUT HER LIFE?

Questions 15-16

(man)	Did you understand what the professor said about the grading in this introductory course?
(woman)	I think so. The professor said that the grades in this course are pass/fail rather than letter grade.
(man)	So, at the end of this course we won't be getting a letter grade like A, B, or C?
(woman)	That's right. At the end of the course, we'll be getting either a pass or a fail, and it takes an average of seventy-five percent or better to pass. With an average lower than seventy-five, the grade is failing.
(man)	Are all the courses in this department graded this way?
(woman)	No, just the introductory course. In all the more advanced courses, letter grades are given, although grades of A are quite hard to come by.

15. *(narrator)* WHAT CAN BE INFERRED ABOUT PASS/FAIL GRADING IN THIS DEPARTMENT?
16. *(narrator)* WHAT IS INDICATED ABOUT THE GRADING IN THE DEPARTMENT?

Questions 17-18

(woman)	Our presentation is tomorrow. Do you think we're ready?
(man)	Well, we've spent so much time preparing and practicing for this presentation. We've got to be ready.
(woman)	I know. For the last two weeks, the only thing we seem to have thought about or talked about is the marketing strategies of Pepsico.
(man)	But this presentation is one-half of our overall grade in the marketing course, so it's really important to prepare for it.
(woman)	That's true. In fact, now that you mention how important the presentation is, perhaps we should practice it one more time.

17. *(narrator)* WHY IS THE PRESENTATION IMPORTANT?
18. *(narrator)* HOW MUCH HAVE THE TWO STUDENTS PREPARED UP TO NOW?

Questions 19-20

(woman)	You're going to take the econometrics course next semester, aren't you? Do you know which section you're going to take?
(man)	I do need to take the econometrics course. How many different sections are there?
(woman)	There are two sections, and each meets for three hours per week. One of the sections is from eight to nine o'clock in the morning three times a week, on Mondays, Wednesdays, and Fridays, and the other section is once a week from seven to ten o'clock on Tuesday evenings.
(man)	Oh, I know which section I'm going to take; that's an easy decision for me. I'm not a morning person, so eight o'clock in the morning sounds awful. It'll be the evening course for me.
(woman)	But the evening course only meets once a week for three hours straight. Don't you think that three hours in a row of this course will be difficult to handle?
(man)	It's better to have three hours in a row in the evening than to have to get up early in the morning three times a week!

19. *(narrator)* WHAT WILL HAPPEN WITH THE ECONOMETRICS COURSE NEXT SEMESTER?
20. *(narrator)* WHAT IS TRUE ABOUT THE MAN?

The Academic Discussions, page 20

Example: ACADEMIC DISCUSSIONS

(narrator)	Listen to a group of students discussing information from a history class. The discussion is on the history of the Statue of Liberty.
(man 1)	❶ First, let's review the historical background of the Statue of Liberty.
(woman)	Good idea. There's going to be a quiz on Friday, and that's one of the topics on Friday's quiz.
(man 2)	The Statue of Liberty is on an island in upper New York Bay. What was the name of the island?
(man 1)	The island used to be known as Bedloe's Island because a man named Isaac Bedloe had owned the island in the seventeenth century. The name was officially changed to Liberty Island in 1956.
(woman)	In the early nineteenth century, a military fort was built on the island to defend New York against military attack. The fort was named Fort Wood, in honor of military hero Eleazar Wood.
(man 2)	So the island was named Bedloe's Island, and the fort on the island was named Fort Wood?
(woman)	Exactly. The fort is a star-shaped construction in the middle of the island. The pedestal of the statue was constructed to rise out of the middle of the star-shaped Fort Wood. ❷ You can see this in the picture in our textbook.
(man)	I believe that the Statue of Liberty was a gift to the American people from the French. The idea for a joint French–American monument to celebrate liberty was proposed, and an organization was established to raise funds and oversee the project.
(woman)	The statue itself was a gift from the French, but the project was more of a joint French–American project. A total of $400,000 was donated by the French people to build the statue, and the American people raised the funds to build the pedestal on which it stands.
(man 2)	And it was a French sculptor who designed the statue? Who was he?
(man 1)	French sculptor Frederic Auguste Bartholdi designed the statue and also oversaw its construction. Did you know that he designed the face of the statue to look like his mother?
(woman)	No, I didn't. That's interesting. The Statue of Liberty has the face of Bartholdi's mother.
(man 1)	❸ When was the statue constructed?
(man 2)	Construction on the statue began in 1875 in Paris. Bartholdi had wanted to have the statue completed for the United States' 1876 centennial celebration, but this turned out to be impossible.
(woman)	But by the time of the centennial celebration in 1876, the right hand and torch had been completed. This part of the statue was sent to the United States for display at centennial celebrations in Philadelphia and New York. Then, at the end of the centennial celebration, this part of the statue was returned to Paris.
(man 2)	And when did the statue finally get delivered?
(woman)	The completed statue was not delivered to the United States until eight years later.
(man 1)	Prior to the arrival of the complete statue in the United States, it was necessary to build a pedestal for the statue. The Americans were responsible for constructing the pedestal the statue stands on.
(man 2)	What are we supposed to know about the pedestal?
(man 1)	American architect Richard Hunt designed the pedestal. The pedestal was built in the middle of the star-shaped Fort Wood. Because of financial problems, it was barely ready for the arrival of the French-built statue in 1884.
(man 2)	So the statue was built in France? How did it get to the United States?
(woman)	The statue had to be taken apart and packed in hundreds of crates in order to be shipped to the United States.
(man 1)	Bartholdi's statue arrived in the United States in its packing crates, and it took a year of work to reassemble the statue on the pedestal that Hunt had designed.
(woman)	I think we've covered that topic enough. Now let's move on to another topic.

1. *(narrator)* WHAT ARE THE STUDENTS PREPARING FOR?
2. *(narrator)* WHAT IS TRUE ABOUT FORT WOOD?
3. *(narrator)* WHAT DID EACH PERSON DO?
4. *(narrator)* THE PROFESSOR EXPLAINS A SERIES OF EVENTS. PUT THE EVENTS IN ORDER.
5. *(narrator)* WHICH PART OF THE STATUE ARRIVED FIRST FROM FRANCE?
6. *(narrator)* IDENTIFY THE ISLAND THAT USED TO BE CALLED BEDLOE'S.

Exercise: ACADEMIC DISCUSSIONS, page 28

Questions 1-5

(narrator) Listen as an instructor leads a discussion of some material from a psychology class. The class was on sleep.

(instructor) ❶ Today, we're going to review the characteristics of sleep, in both humans and other types of living beings. First of all, what are the main characteristics of sleep? What happens to the human body when a person is sleeping? Pam?

(Pam) ❷ Well, during sleep, the muscles relax, both breathing and heart rate slow down, and brain waves change.

(instructor) Exactly. Now, Ron, can you explain how brain waves change?

(Ron) ❸ The brain of a person who is awake and relaxed gives off about ten small waves per second. In deep sleep, however, the brain waves become much slower and larger, with the slowest and largest during the first few hours of a period of sleep. This is called the period of slow-wave sleep.

(instructor) Are brains waves always large and slow during sleep? Nick?

(Nick) ❹ No, there are periods of small and fast waves at intervals during a period of sleep. These short and fast waves are similar to the brain waves of a person who is awake.

(instructor) What happens to the eyes during these periods of fast brain activity?

(Pam) ❺ The sleeper's eyes move rapidly. This is called "rapid-eye-movement sleep" or REM sleep.

(instructor) Yes, Pam, exactly. And what other name does this period of REM, or rapid-eye-movement, sleep have?

(Pam) REM sleep is also called "dreaming sleep" because this is when dreaming occurs.

(instructor) Okay, so we have seen that when a person sleeps, there are different types of brain wave activity. There are periods of large, slow brain waves during deep sleep, and there are periods of small, fast brain waves during REM, or dreaming, sleep....Now, we're going to compare human sleep patterns with the sleep patterns of certain animals. What can you tell me about the sleep patterns of mammals, Ron?

(Ron) Mammals seem to experience true sleep, with changes in brain wave patterns. They have periods of dreaming sleep and periods of slow-wave sleep.

(instructor) Do birds experience sleep in the same way?

(Ron) Birds also experience sleep with changes in brain wave patterns, but they have only very brief periods of dreaming sleep.

(instructor) And what about reptiles and fish? Nick?

(Nick) Reptiles also experience sleep with changes in brain wave patterns, but they do not seem to have periods of dreaming sleep. Fish have periods when they become less aware of their surroundings, but there is no scientific evidence of changes in brain waves.

(instructor) Excellent. Now, Pam, let's see if you can summarize the information for us. Which types of animals seem to experience changes in brain waves while they are sleeping?

(Pam) Humans, of course, and also mammals, birds, and reptiles. Fish do not seem to experience changes in brain waves.

(instructor) And what about periods of dreaming?

(Pam) Again, humans, of course, experience periods of dreaming, and most mammals seem to experience the same type of dreaming, with periods of dreaming sleep and periods of slow-wave sleep. Birds may experience short periods of dreaming, but reptiles and fish do not.

(instructor) That's very good, and that's all for today. I'll see you all again next week.

1. *(narrator)* WHAT HAPPENS DURING HUMAN SLEEP?
2. *(narrator)* WHAT TYPES OF BRAIN ACTIVITY ARE COMMON DURING HUMAN SLEEP?
3. *(narrator)* IDENTIFY THE ANIMAL THAT PROBABLY HAS CHANGES IN BRAIN ACTIVITY DURING SLEEP BUT DOES NOT DREAM.
4. *(narrator)* HOW LONG ARE THE PERIODS OF DREAMING FOR EACH OF THESE ANIMALS?
5. *(narrator)* IDENTIFY THE PART OF THE BRAIN WAVE PATTERN WHEN DREAMING TAKES PLACE.

Questions 6-10

(narrator) Listen to a group of students discussing a report for a history class. The report is on the history of eyeglasses.

(woman) ❶ Look at this book. It's got good information and good pictures.
(man) What's it about?

(woman)	It's about different types of eyeglasses through the ages. Maybe we can use some of this information as part of our report for history class.
(man)	Let's see....Look at all these different types of eyeglasses and reading devices. Many of the ones here are several hundred years old. How long have eyeglasses been around? Does the book have that information?
(woman)	The book says that eyeglasses were known to exist in the late 1200s. But the earliest eyeglasses must have been difficult to use because there was no way to wear them. People just had to hold the eyeglasses up to their eyes when they wanted to read or to look at something tiny.
(man)	It wasn't until the 1700s that there were the sort of modern eyeglasses with frames that sit on the nose and ears to prop them up. That's so much more convenient than holding glasses up to your eyes.
(woman)	The book says that even though eyeglasses with frames were invented in the 1720s, they didn't really catch on until much later, and until they became fashionable, a bunch of rather unusual types of glasses were common. Look at some of these pictures.
(man)	❷ This woman looks like she's holding a small telescope.
(woman)	It does look like a telescope, doesn't it? It's called a prospect glass, and it was quite fashionable in the 1600s. It magnified things in the same way that a telescope does.
(man)	It must have been rather uncomfortable to have to hold a prospect glass up to your eye whenever you wanted to read.
(woman)	You're right. I can't imagine reading for long periods of time like that.
(man)	❸ These next two were fashionable in the 1800s. The man is wearing a monocle, and the woman is holding something called a lorgnette.
(woman)	The eyepiece that the man is wearing must be called a monocle because it only covers one eye....How do you think the monocle stays in place in the man's eye? There doesn't seem to be anything holding it in place.
(man)	The man had to hold the monocle in place by squeezing the muscles around the eye.
(woman)	That couldn't have been comfortable for long periods of time.
(man)	I'm sure it wasn't....Now, look at the woman. She's from the same period as the man, the 1800s. During this period, a man would use a monocle to see, and a woman would use a lorgnette.
(woman)	The lorgnette had a long handle, so a woman had to hold the glasses up to her eyes by the handle in order to read. The lorgnette doesn't look as hard on the eyes as the monocle is on the man's eyes, but it had to be uncomfortable for a woman to hold the glasses up to her eyes for long periods of time while she tried to read.
(man)	But at least she didn't have to grasp the glasses with the muscles around her eye, and she had glasses covering both her eyes. The lorgnette looks a bit more usable than the monocle.
(woman)	Very honestly, none of these older eyeglasses looks very comfortable. But we did get a good overall view of the development of eyeglasses.
(man)	Now, let's think about what type of information we're going to include in our report.

6.	(narrator)	HOW LONG ARE EYEGLASSES KNOWN TO HAVE BEEN IN USE?
7.	(narrator)	WHAT ARE THE VARIOUS TYPES OF EYE PIECES?
8.	(narrator)	SELECT THE EYE PIECE THAT WOULD MOST LIKELY HAVE BEEN USED BY A NINETEENTH CENTURY WOMAN.
9.	(narrator)	THE STUDENTS DISCUSS A SERIES OF HISTORICAL EVENTS. PUT THE EVENTS IN ORDER.
10.	(narrator)	HOW DO THE SPEAKERS COMPARE THE OLDER VERSIONS OF EYEGLASSES TO TODAY'S EYEGLASSES?

Questions 11-15

(narrator)	Listen to a group of students discussing some material from an oceanography lecture. The lecture was on changes in sea level.
(man 1)	❶ Does anyone want to go over this lecture on changes in sea level? It was really hard for me to understand this material from our oceanography class, and I'm not sure if my notes are very clear.
(woman)	That sounds like a good idea to me. I think I understood most of it, but I really would like to make sure that I have good notes.
(man 2)	Could I join in, too? I really need some help with this.
(man 1)	This is great. Maybe if we work together, it'll all be clear....Now, the professor was talking about different types of changes in sea level, and I think he talked about three different types.

(woman)	No, it was four different types, I believe.
(man 1)	What were these four different types of changes in sea level? I understood when he talked about waves and swells, but after that I got kind of lost.
(man 2)	He also talked about storm surges. I think I understood about that part.
(woman)	Yes, and the other type of change in sea level was a *tsunami* or tidal wave.
(man 1)	*Tsunami?* How do you spell that?
(woman)	T...S...U...N...A...M...I. It's a Japanese word that is used fairly commonly in English now. It means "high water in the harbor" in Japanese.
(man 1)	Okay, so the professor talked about four different types of changes in sea level. ❷ Let me write this in my notes. The four different types of changes in sea level are waves, swells, storm surges, and *tsunamis.* Is that it?
(woman)	Yeah. You got it.
(man 2)	Now that we've figured out how many there are, it would be great if we could get clear on what they each are.
(man 1)	All right, let me start because I think I understood the first two. Waves are created when wind moves over the surface of the water. Then, a swell occurs when waves have travelled a long way from the wind that created them.
(man 2)	So, waves occur in the wind, and swells result when the waves have moved away from the wind.
(woman)	That's right. And because waves are right in the wind, they tend to be jagged and rough. Swells, on the other hand, become smooth and symmetrical because they are far from the wind.
(man 2)	Okay, now, the third type of change in sea level is a storm surge. A storm surge occurs in a combination of strong winds and low atmospheric pressure during a storm.
(woman)	The storm surge actually forms when the water is pushed ahead of the wind into areas with rising pressure. When a storm surge hits a coastline, the water can rise considerably above the normal coastline and cause flooding.
(man 1)	So the flooding that results from a big storm, a hurricane, or a typhoon actually is the result of a storm surge.
(woman)	Yes. That's right. Now, the last type of change in sea level is a *tsunami* or tidal wave.
(man 1)	Those are two names for the same thing? Or are they two different things?
(woman)	They're the same. They don't result from the wind on the surface of the ocean; instead, they start on the ocean floor with an underwater earthquake.
(man 2)	Then, why are they called tidal waves if they're caused by earthquakes and not tides?
(woman)	They were given the name tidal wave before their cause was really understood. They were thought to be caused by high tides, so they were named tidal waves. Now, they're known to be caused by earthquakes and are probably more often referred to as *tsunamis.*
(man 1)	Well, that really helps me. I understand this all a whole lot better now. Thanks very much. See you later.
(woman)	Bye for now.
(man 2)	See you later.

11. *(narrator)* WHEN DO THE STUDENTS HAVE THIS CONVERSATION?
12. *(narrator)* IDENTIFY THE WAVE THAT IS MOST PROBABLY A SWELL.
13. *(narrator)* WHAT IS TRUE ABOUT STORM SURGES?
14. *(narrator)* WHAT IS THE CAUSE OF EACH OF THESE CHANGES IN SEA LEVEL?
15. *(narrator)* THE STUDENTS DESCRIBE THE PROCESS OF A STORM SURGE. SUMMARIZE THE PROCESS BY PUTTING THE EVENTS IN ORDER.

The Academic Lectures, page 34

Example: ACADEMIC LECTURES

(narrator)	Listen to a lecture in a biology class. The professor is talking about food chains.
(professor)	❶ A food chain refers to the process in nature by which animals are fed by other animals and plants. All animals are ultimately dependent on plants for food: some animals eat plants directly, while other animals eat animals that eat plants. In this way, food chains develop.
	A simple food chain consists of one producer, one primary consumer, and one secondary consumer. ❷ Look at this diagram of a simple food chain. In such a food chain, a producer is always a plant, and that plant is eaten by a primary consumer, which is a plant-eating animal called a herbivore. The primary consumer is eaten by a secondary consumer, a meat-eating an-

imal called a carnivore. An example of a simple food chain would start with grass, which is eaten by a rabbit, which is then eaten by a fox.

A more complicated food chain can have more than one secondary consumer, or carnivore. In this type of food chain, one meat-eating carnivore devours the plant-eating herbivore, and another meat-eating carnivore devours the first meat-eating carnivore. ❸ Look at this example of a more complicated food chain. This example begins with grasses, which are eaten by the plant-eating antelope. At the next stage of the food chain, the antelope is eaten by the carnivorous lion, which then can be devoured by a second carnivore in the food chain, such as a vulture. There cannot be more than one producer in a complicated food chain because one plant does not eat another, and there cannot be more than one primary consumer because one plant-eating animal does not eat another plant-eating animal. However, a food chain can have a number of secondary consumers, carnivores that feast on lower animals in the food chain.

A further complication to some food chains is that one animal can enter the food chain at various stages. This means that one animal can enter a food chain as either a primary consumer, a herbivore, or as a secondary consumer, a carnivore. ❹ Now we will look at an example of a food chain in which one of the animals enters the food chain twice. This food chain begins with grasses, which can be eaten by the plant-eating rabbit. A baboon can be part of this food chain as either a primary or a secondary consumer. As a primary consumer, it feeds on the grasses, and as a secondary consumer, it feeds on the rabbit. A leopard can also be part of this food chain as a secondary consumer that feeds on the baboon.

1. *(narrator)*   WHAT HAPPENS IN A SIMPLE FOOD CHAIN?
2. *(narrator)*   WHAT HAPPENS IN A COMPLICATED FOOD CHAIN?
3. *(narrator)*   DESCRIBE THE COMPONENTS OF A FOOD CHAIN.
4. *(narrator)*   THE PROFESSOR EXPLAINS A PROCESS. SUMMARIZE THE PROCESS BY PUTTING THE EVENTS IN ORDER.
5. *(narrator)*   WHICH ONE OF THESE IS MOST LIKELY A HERBIVORE?
6. *(narrator)*   IDENTIFY THE PRODUCER IN THE DIAGRAM.

Exercise: ACADEMIC LECTURES, page 41

Questions 1-5

(narrator)   Listen to a lecture in an astronomy class. The professor is talking about the moons of Jupiter.

(professor)   ❶ We have finished our discussion of the rings that surround the planet Jupiter, and now we will move on to a discussion of Jupiter's moons, of which there are sixteen.

The four largest of Jupiter's sixteen known moons are called the Galilean satellites. This group of four moons was named after one of their discovers, Galileo Galilei, who first spotted them early in the seventeenth century. These four Galilean satellites are named Io, Europa, Ganymede, and Callisto, and they are all remarkably different. ❷ Look at the diagram showing Jupiter and the four Gallilean moons. Io is the closest of these four moons to the planet Jupiter. Io is characterized by the continuous volcanic eruptions that result from the strong gravitational interaction that it has with Jupiter. The second of the moons in distance from Jupiter and the second largest of the moons is Europa. Unlike the volcanic surface of Io, the surface of Europa is flat and smooth. Scientists have suggested that the smooth surface of the moon Europa could be due to a melting and refreezing of its icy surface. The third of these four moons from Jupiter is Ganymede, which is the largest of Jupiter's moons and the largest and heaviest satellite in our solar system. Its diameter is 5262 kilometers (or 3270 miles), larger than the diameter of the planet Mercury, and its mass is more than 2000 times greater than the mass of our Moon. The outermost of the four Galilean satellites is Calisto, which is heavily marked with craters. According to scientists, these craters could have resulted from earlier violent impacts with space objects.

We see that these four largest of Jupiter's moons, Io, Europa, Ganymede, and Callisto, are all quite distinct. ❸ Now, we are moving on to the remaining twelve of Jupiter's moons. The twelve other moons of Jupiter are all quite small, and they are clustered in three groups of four. One group of four tiny moons is quite close to Jupiter, and the other two groups of four are much farther out from the planet. These outermost groups of moons are thought to be captured asteroids that have been pulled into orbit around Jupiter.

Well, that is all for our study of the planet Jupiter. In the next lecture, we will begin our study of the next planet in our solar system, Saturn.

1. *(narrator)* HOW MANY GALILEAN SATELLITES ARE THERE AROUND JUPITER?
2. *(narrator)* HOW ARE THESE MOONS CHARACTERIZED?
3. *(narrator)* IDENTIFY THE BODIES THAT SCIENTISTS BELIEVE MAY BE CAPTURED ASTEROIDS.
4. *(narrator)* SELECT THE MOON THAT MOST CLOSELY RESEMBLES CALLISTO.
5. *(narrator)* WHAT WILL BE THE TOPIC OF THE NEXT LECTURE?

Questions 6-10

(narrator) Listen to a lecture in a music class. The professor is talking about the trumpet.

(professor) ❶ The trumpet of today, with its long oblong loop of metal and three piston valves, is a brass instrument that has a commanding role in modern-day bands and orchestras. This modern musical instrument has a long and interesting history. As we take a look at the development of the trumpet, you should keep the following points about the trumpet in mind. ❷ First, the trumpet is a universal instrument that has been part of numerous cultures. Second, the trumpet has undergone numerous mutations in its development. Third, the trumpet has served a variety of purposes in its various mutations and different cultures.

The first point that we want to understand about the trumpet is that many early cultures had their own distinct version of a trumpet, so it is difficult to say that the trumpet originated in one specific culture. Early cultures in Africa and Australia had trumpetlike hollow tubes, and by 1400 B.C. the Egyptians had developed wide-belled trumpets made from bronze and silver. Assyrian, Greek, Etruscan, Roman, Celtic, and Teutonic civilizations all had some form of the trumpet, and during the Crusades in the Middle Ages, the Europeans were introduced to the Arab *trumpa*.

The second point to understand about the trumpet is that it has undergone extensive changes in construction, both in the materials used and in the shape. ❸ In this drawing, you can see various types of trumpets that have been used throughout the ages. Some of the materials that have been used to construct trumpets have been the cane plant, horns or tusks of animals, and metals such as bronze, silver, and brass. In shape, the trumpet began as a long, hollow, straight tube to which a wide-mouthed bell was later added to magnify the sound. Then, as the tubing got longer and longer, it was bent to make the instrument more convenient, first into an S-shape and then into the circling loop of today. To increase the number and accuracy of tones produced, keys and a slide similar to the slide on a trombone were added to the trumpet before the three piston valves of the modern trumpet became the norm.

❹ The third point to understand about the trumpet is that it has served a variety of purposes. The trumpet has only relatively recently been considered a musical instrument. For most of its long history, it has been used in other ways. First, the trumpet has been used for ceremonial purposes, perhaps to herald the arrival of an important personage or to provide resonant ornamentation during a celebration or rite. In addition, the trumpet has been used for communication over distance; ancient versions of the trumpet with a limited range of low powerful notes were used for communication from village to village and from mountaintop to mountaintop. Finally, the trumpet has been used by numerous cultures in battle, to announce the charge into battle and to exhort troops to fight more intensely during battle. It was not until the last few centuries, when changes and improvements to the trumpet made it more versatile, that it became established in its role as a musical instrument.

6. *(narrator)* WHAT IS TRUE ABOUT THE DEVELOPMENT OF THE TRUMPET?
7. *(narrator)* THE PROFESSOR EXPLAINS THE DEVELOPMENT OF THE TRUMPET. PUT THE TYPES OF TRUMPETS IN THE ORDER IN WHICH THEY WERE DEVELOPED.
8. *(narrator)* WHICH WAS NOT MENTIONED AS A MATERIAL FROM WHICH TRUMPETS HAVE BEEN MADE?
9. *(narrator)* IDENTIFY THE TRUMPET WITH THE MOST ACCURATE TONES.
10. *(narrator)* HOW DID THE LECTURER CATEGORIZE EACH OF THESE USES OF A TRUMPET?

Questions 11-15

(narrator)   Listen to a lecture in a geography class. The professor is talking about the formation of mountains.

(professor)   ❶ Today we'll be discussing the formation of various mountain ranges around the world. We'll be discussing the major mountain chains such as the Himalayas, the Rockies, the Alps, and the Andes. We'll also be discussing the development of two North American chains, the Appalachians and the Cascades, which do not rank among the world's tallest. The development of these two ranges, when compared with the development of the Himalayas, Rockies, Andes, and Alps, provides a clear overall picture of the evolutionary process of the development of mountain ranges.

❷ Look at the world map showing the mountain ranges of the world. The tall mountain ranges of today's world were all formed within the last hundred million years. The Rocky Mountains began forming about a hundred million years ago and today comprise a 3,300 mile range. The Andes began forming about 65 million years ago, through volcanic activity. The Andes are actually part of the volcanically active Ring of Fire that encircles the Pacific Ocean. This range is more than a thousand miles longer than the Rockies. The Alps and the Himalayas are actually both part of the same 7,000-mile mountain system. They began forming about 80 million years ago from the crashing action of major tectonic plates.

❸ If you were asked to name the world's major mountain ranges, you might not think of the Appalachians. As you can see from the map, the Appalachians are a range of north–south running mountains in the eastern part of North America. These mountains are actually far older than the major mountain ranges of today, the Himalayas, the Alps, the Andes, the Rockies, and in all probability the Appalachians used to be just as big and majestic. The Appalachians began forming more than 400 million years ago and were completely formed 200 million years ago, more than 100 million years before the Rockies began forming. The Appalachians were formed during major collisions of the North American Plate with others of the world's great plates. At their height, the Appalachians were a grand and impressive mountain range, perhaps rivaling the Himalayas of today. Over millions of years, however, these mountains have been eroded by the forces of nature and no longer have the impressive height they used to.

❹ Before we wrap up for today, I'd like to add one final note about the Cascade Mountains. You can see from the map that the Cascades are in the western part of North America. These mountains completed their rise from the sea scarcely a million years ago and are among the youngest of the world's mountain ranges. They are volcanic mountains that are also part of the volcanically active Ring of Fire encircling the Pacific Ocean.

That's all for today. I hope that this lecture has helped you to understand the evolution of the mountains of the earth. You will find additional details on this topic in the assigned reading in the textbook.

11. (narrator)   THE PROFESSOR EXPLAINS THE ORDER IN WHICH MOUNTAIN RANGES DEVELOPED. PUT THE RANGES IN THE ORDER IN WHICH THEY DEVELOPED.
12. (narrator)   WHICH OF THE FOLLOWING MOUNTAIN RANGES ARE PART OF THE RING OF FIRE?
13. (narrator)   HOW LONG IS EACH OF THE MOUNTAIN RANGES?
14. (narrator)   IDENTIFY THE MOUNTAIN RANGE THAT IS PREDOMINANTLY VOLCANIC IN ORIGIN.
15. (narrator)   WHAT IS TRUE ABOUT THE APPALACHIANS, ACCORDING TO THE LECTURER?

TOEFL® Computer-Based Test: The Listening Section, page 47

1. (woman)   Are you going to the conference tonight?
   (man)   Yes, indeed. I wouldn't miss it.
   (woman)   Will Dr. Burton be the speaker at tonight's conference?
   (man)   As far as I know.
   (narrator)   WHAT CAN BE INFERRED ABOUT THE MAN?

2. (man)   I'm going to stop in at this shop and get a couple of magazines to read.
   (woman)   But the plane is taking off soon.
   (narrator)   WHAT DOES THE WOMAN MEAN?

3. *(man)*   The fee for this course is one hundred dollars.
   (woman)   How can the fee be a hundred dollars? It wasn't that much last semester.
   (narrator) WHAT DOES THE WOMAN SAY ABOUT THE COURSE?

4. *(man)*   How serious was the accident?
   (woman)   Well, the motorcycle rider was taken to the hospital in an ambulance.
   (narrator) WHAT DOES THE WOMAN MEAN?

5. *(woman)*   Can you finish this project within the next two hours?
   (man)   What you're asking for is not impossible.
   (narrator) WHAT DOES THE MAN MEAN?

6. *(woman)*   I can't believe it actually snowed here. We rarely get snow this far south.
   (man)   I wish it had been a little colder. Then the snow might have stuck around longer.
   (narrator) WHAT DOES THE MAN MEAN?

7. *(man)*   I just spent the afternoon at the new art gallery.
   (woman)   What did you think of it?
   (man)   I couldn't have been more impressed!
   (narrator) WHAT DOES THE MAN SAY ABOUT THE ART GALLERY?

8. *(woman)*   I didn't realize before how tall this building is.
   (man)   There can't be too many more flights of stairs to go.
   (woman)   If only the elevator hadn't been broken. Then we wouldn't have had to climb all those stairs.
   (narrator) WHAT DOES THE WOMAN IMPLY?

9. *(woman)*   I've got to get over to the chemistry lab. There are only a couple more hours until the lab closes, and I've still got a lot more to do.
   (man)   So you haven't finished the lab assignment yet!
   (narrator) WHAT HAD THE MAN ASSUMED ABOUT THE WOMAN?

Questions 10-11

   (man)   We'd better hurry to the bookstore now. I think it's going to close in about an hour.
   (woman)   Then, we'd better get there soon. We need to get the texts for sociology and start reading them tonight.
   (man)   The teaching assistant said that we're going to need three books overall for the course: the main text, the workbook, and the study guide.
   (woman)   He said that the text and the workbook are required and the study guide is optional. I think I'm going to get all three.
   (man)   Me, too. I need all the help I can get. Now, let's get to the bookstore before it closes.
   (woman)   Good idea....But, you know, after we buy all these books, we actually have to read them.

10. *(narrator)* WHY ARE THE STUDENTS IN A HURRY?
11. *(narrator)* WHICH BOOKS MUST THE STUDENTS HAVE FOR THE SOCIOLOGY COURSE?

Questions 12-13

   (man)   Have you finished your paper for Friday yet?
   (woman)   No, it's not really a long paper, and it's not due for two more days. I should have plenty of time to finish it.
   (man)   The professor said that she wanted three to five pages, didn't she?
   (woman)   Yes, three to five pages, typed and double-spaced. She said she wouldn't accept anything handwritten.
   (man)   That's not the problem for me; I can get three to five pages typed on my computer in no time. My problem is that I just don't have enough ideas on the topic to fill those pages.
   (woman)   I guess you'd better get working on the paper. With only two days left until the paper's due, there's not much time.

12. *(narrator)* ON WHAT DAY DOES THIS CONVERSATION PROBABLY TAKE PLACE?
13. *(narrator)* WHAT IS TRUE ABOUT THE PAPER?

Questions 14-17

(narrator)   Listen to a lecture in a history class. The professor is talking about the state of Franklin.

(professor)   ❶ In a list of the states in the United States, have you ever heard of the state of Franklin? Most citizens of the United States would swear that there was no such state. Of course, the state of Franklin doesn't exist today, but it actually was a reality in the country's earlier days, in the period of time soon after the end of the American Revolution in 1783 but before George Washington became the country's first president.

The state of Franklin, named in honor of American statesman Benjamin Franklin, existed for the four-year period from 1784 until 1788. ❷ Let's look at the map. In 1784, the state government of North Carolina felt unable to take care of its vast territories, and it voted to return some of its western lands to the federal government. Some of the citizens of the area that was no longer part of North Carolina met together and declared their territory the state of Franklin because they did not have a state government. They immediately began doing business as a state in spite of the fact that the federal government had not recognized their state. They elected a governor, they set up laws and courts, and they began collecting taxes as a state.

One year later, in 1785, the state of North Carolina reversed itself and decided that it wanted to keep these territories operating as part of the state of North Carolina. For several years, there was a very unstable situation in Franklin with two dueling state governments asserting control, and both governments running courts, enforcing laws, and trying to collect taxes. After a four-year period of tumult and confusion, North Carolina governor Richard Caswell was able to resolve the differences between North Carolina and Franklin, and Franklin's four years of partial statehood came to an end.

❸ Now, before we wrap up for the day, let's review the chronology of events in the lecture. In 1783, a treaty was signed between the United States and England to end the Revolutionary War. The period of time after the war was primarily a period of organization for the new country. In 1784, the people of Franklin declared themselves a state separate from the state of North Carolina; a period of confusion and tumult in government lasted for four years until 1788, when Franklin was reunited with North Carolina. All of this actually took place before George Washington was elected the first president of the United States in 1789.

14. *(narrator)*   WHEN WAS FRANKLIN A STATE?
15. *(narrator)*   WHAT CAUSED THE CITIZENS OF FRANKLIN TO DECLARE STATEHOOD?
16. *(narrator)*   WHAT HAPPENED IN THE PERIOD OF TIME JUST AFTER FRANKLIN DECLARED ITSELF A STATE?
17. *(narrator)*   THE PROFESSOR DESCRIBES A SERIES OF HISTORICAL EVENTS. PUT THE EVENTS IN ORDER.

Questions 18-19

(man)   Here I am in trouble again.
(woman)   What's the problem?
(man)   The same problem that I always have — procrastination. I have an exam tomorrow, and I meant to start studying early, but I just never got around to it. Now I'll have to study all night tonight.
(woman)   So you're a procrastinator!
(man)   One of the worst!
(woman)   You just need to come up with a study plan and stick to it no matter what happens.
(man)   That's always what I intend to do, but it just doesn't seem to happen. It's easier said than done.

18. *(narrator)*   WHAT IS THE MAN'S PROBLEM?
19. *(narrator)*   WHAT DOES THE WOMAN SUGGEST TO THE MAN?

Questions 20-25

(narrator)   Listen to a discussion by a group of students taking an anatomy class. They are discussing the bones of the human body.

(man 1)   ❶ Do you want to get together and go over some of the materials for anatomy class? We might have a quiz today.
(woman)   There are an awful lot of quizzes in this class, aren't there? I've never been in a course with so many quizzes.

(man 2)	That's true. Some professors don't give any quizzes at all. But in this course, we seem to have a quiz in just about every class.
(man 1)	Then, we'd better start discussing the material because there's probably going to be a quiz today, and class starts in about an hour.
(woman)	What was the reading about? Oh, I remember; it was about the bones in the human body. ❷ Look at this diagram of the bones in the human body. We have a whole lot to learn.
(man 2)	That's right. I believe that there are two hundred and six bones in the human body.
(man 1)	Well, that's sort of right. There may be two hundred and six bones in the adult human body, but babies actually have many more than two hundred and six bones — babies can have as many as three hundred bones.
(woman)	I don't understand how that can happen. How can babies have more bones than adults? The bones don't disappear, do they?
(man 2)	No, they don't disappear. They fuse.
(man 1)	They fuse? Does that mean that they grow together?
(man 2)	Yes, it does. So a baby can be born with up to three hundred bones, but as the baby grows, the bones also grow, and they can grow together, or fuse.
(woman)	Have you ever noticed the soft spot on the top of the head of a very young baby? The spot is soft because there's no bone there.
(man 1)	But there will eventually be bone there....❸ See... In this drawing of a baby's skull, there's no bone on the top of the head, but in the drawing of the adult's skull, the two pieces of the skull have joined together into one bone.
(woman)	Yes. The two pieces of the skull join together into one bone.
(man 1)	Approximately when do these two bones grow together? Do you know?
(woman)	By the time a baby is a year and a half old, the two bones have grown together.
(man 2)	What about all the other bones in the body?
(woman)	The last bone in the human body to fuse is the collarbone.
(man 1)	So when the collarbone has fused, there are two hundred and six bones left? By what age does this happen?
(man 2)	Didn't the chapter say that bone growth was complete by the age of fifteen?
(woman)	Wait... I thought that the chapter said that bone growth could continue until the age of twenty-five, not fifteen. Do either of you know?
(man 2)	I'm not sure. Let me look it up... Here it is... The chapter says "Bone growth in humans may end as early as the age of fifteen or continue as late as the age of twenty-five." So we both were a little right.
(woman)	Actually, we both were a little wrong. I don't think we would've been able to answer a question about that correctly on a quiz. But now we can, and that's what's important because class starts in just a little bit.
(man 1)	I actually hope that we do have a quiz today; I feel ready for one.
(man 2)	Me, too. Come on. Let's head for class now.

20.	(narrator)	HOW OFTEN ARE QUIZZES GIVEN IN THE ANATOMY CLASS THAT THESE STUDENTS ARE TAKING?
21.	(narrator)	HOW MANY BONES ARE THERE IN THE HUMAN BODY?
22.	(narrator)	WHAT HAPPENS TO SOME OF A BABY'S BONES AS THE BABY GROWS?
23.	(narrator)	WHAT HAPPENS TO A BABY BY THE AGE OF A YEAR AND A HALF?
24.	(narrator)	IDENTIFY THE FINAL BONE IN THE BODY TO FUSE.
25.	(narrator)	BY WHAT AGE IS BONE GROWTH IN HUMANS COMPLETE?

Questions 26-30

(narrator)	Listen to a lecture in a business class. The professor is talking about the early days of the IBM Corporation.
(professor)	❶ In this part of the course, we have been looking at the early history of some of today's major corporations. We've already looked at the early history of the Coca-Cola® Company, the Ford Motor Corporation, and Sears and Roebuck. Today, we're going to look at the development of IBM, which had its roots in a most unusual set of events.
	❷ In the nineteenth-century American West, the primary mode of mass transportation was the railroad, and a serious problem that plagued U.S. trains was a proliferation of train robberies. Trains were easy targets for robbers because they moved on set schedules along set tracks through isolated areas. A commonly used and successful method for holding up a train was for a gang of outlaws to place some of its members on a targeted train as ticketed passen-

gers and have the rest of the gang waiting on horseback in a predetermined location far removed from civilization, law officers, and means of communication. When the train arrived at the appointed spot, the gang members on board pulled out weapons, stopped the train for their waiting cohorts, robbed the train and its passengers, and escaped on horseback.

To most of you, this story probably does not sound much like the early history of the IBM Corporation. Can any of you imagine what train robberies in the American West had to do with the development of this major corporation?

❸ To deal with the huge number of train robberies, it was proposed to the railroads that they record the physical characteristics of passengers on the tickets at the time of purchase. The physical characteristics could be recorded by punching holes in appropriate spots on the tickets. Then, if a particular passenger who had purchased a ticket turned out to be a train robber, the ticket could be used by law officials to obtain a physical description of the robber.

This idea to prevent train robberies was never used extensively, but it did provide statistician Herman Hollerith with an idea for collecting census information from U.S. citizens. For the 1890 U.S. census, Hollerith developed a tabulating machine that could be used to read cards on which holes had been punched to describe characteristics of citizens. Because of Hollerith's tabulating machine, the 1890 census proceeded far more quickly, accurately, and effortlessly than had any previous census.

Six years after the 1890 census, Hollerith founded the Tabulating Machine Company, and a few decades later the Tabulating Machine Company became the foundation of the International Business Machines Corporation, or IBM.

We can see from the example of IBM, and from the examples we've heard about in previous lectures, that many of today's largest and most successful corporations actually grew from tiny seeds of ideas.

26. *(narrator)* WHAT COMPANIES HAVE ALREADY BEEN DISCUSSED IN THE COURSE?
27. *(narrator)* THE PROFESSOR DESCRIBES A SERIES OF EVENTS. PUT THE EVENTS IN ORDER.
28. *(narrator)* WHAT PROPOSED SOLUTION TO THE PROBLEM OF TRAIN ROBBERS DID THE LECTURER DISCUSS?
29. *(narrator)* HOW WAS THE MACHINE THAT HOLLERITH DEVELOPED USED?
30. *(narrator)* IN WHAT YEAR DID EACH OF THESE EVENTS OCCUR?

Answer Key: THE LISTENING SECTION

> The first number following each question indicates the correct answer to the question, and the number in parentheses indicates the skill number (from the *Longman Student CD-ROM*) of the question.

Pre-Test: SHORT DIALOGUES

1.	1	(1)	7.	3	(7)	13.	4	(13)
2.	4	(2)	8.	1	(8)	14.	4	(14)
3.	1	(3)	9.	4	(9)	15.	3	(15)
4.	2	(4)	10.	2	(10)	16.	1	(16)
5.	1	(5)	11.	3	(11)	17.	2	(17)
6.	4	(6)	12.	3	(12)			

Post-Test: SHORT DIALOGUES

1.	3	(1)	7.	2	(7)	13.	3	(13)
2.	4	(2)	8.	2	(8)	14.	1	(14)
3.	3	(3)	9.	3	(9)	15.	4	(15)
4.	3	(4)	10.	2	(10)	16.	3	(16)
5.	2	(5)	11.	4	(11)	17.	4	(17)
6.	4	(6)	12.	1	(12)			

Exercise: CASUAL CONVERSATIONS

1.	2	8.	4	15.	2
2.	3	9.	4	16.	4
3.	1	10.	2	17.	3
4.	4	11.	1	18.	2
5.	1	12.	2	19.	1
6.	4	13.	1	20.	4
7.	3	14.	3		

Exercise: ACADEMIC DISCUSSIONS

1. 3
2. 1, 4
3. C
4. *fish, birds, mammals*
5. C
6. 2
7. *lorgnette, prospect glass, monocle*
8. C
9. *The first eyeglasses were invented.*
   Monocles were fashionable.
   Prospect glasses were fashionable.
   Framed eyeglasses became fashionable.
10. 3
11. D
12. B
13. 1, 2
14. *waves, storm surges, tsunamis*
15. *Low pressure and winds cause a storm.*
    The winds push water ahead of the storm.
    The surge hits the coastline.
    Flooding ensues.

Exercise: ACADEMIC LECTURES

1. 2
2. *Ganymede, Io, Europa*
3. D
4. C
5. 1
6. 2, 3
7. *A long, straight tube*
   The addition of a bell
   Tubing in a circular loop
   The addition of valves

8. 2
9. D
10. *communication, battle, ceremony*
11. *Appalachians, Rockies, Andes, Cascades*
12. 1, 4
13. *Rockies, Andes, Alps*
14. A
15. 1, 4

TOEFL® COMPUTER-BASED TEST: THE LISTENING SECTION

1. 2   (12)
2. 4   (2)
3. 3   (7)
4. 2   (5)
5. 3   (8)
6. 1   (14)
7. 2   (10)
8. 1   (15)
9. 3   (13)
10. 4
11. 2
12. 2
13. 3
14. 4
15. 2
16. 3,4
17. *The Revolutionary War ended.*
    Franklin declared itself a state.
    Franklin united with North Carolina.
    George Washington was elected president.

18. 3
19. 2
20. 4
21. 1, 2
22. 3
23. 2
24. B
25. 4
26. 2, 4
27. *The train went to an isolated area.*
    Ticketed passengers on board stopped the
      train.
    Waiting robbers boarded the train.
    The robbers all escaped on horseback.
28. C
29. 2
30. *IBM was founded: 1924*
    The Tabulating Machine Company was
      started: 1896
    A census was run by Hollerith: 1890

Answer Key: THE STRUCTURE SECTION

The first number following each question number indicates the correct answer to the question, and the number in parentheses indicates the skill number (from the *Longman Student CD-ROM*) of the question. The word or expression in italics indicates a possible correction of the error.

Diagnostic Pre-Test: THE STRUCTURE SECTION

1.	3	(27)	*largest*		31.	3	(54)	*history*
2.	2	(30)	*returned*		32.	2	(13)	
3.	1	(1)			33.	4	(60)	*another*
4.	3	(32)	*remain*		34.	2	(35)	*was*
5.	4	(39)	*nostril*		35.	4	(44)	*their*
6.	2	(2)			36.	1	(8)	
7.	3	(43)	*him*		37.	1	(55)	*the*
8.	2	(21)	*have*		38.	4	(26)	*there is*
9.	2	(6)			39.	4	(9)	
10.	4	(33)	*was*		40.	2	(22)	*slopes is*
11.	1	(40)	*many*		41.	4	(15)	
12.	2	(23)	*represents*		42.	3	(57)	*introduced to*
13.	3	(7)			43.	1	(14)	
14.	3	(31)	*fed*		44.	4	(11)	
15.	4	(34)	*have been*		45.	1	(48)	*normally develop*
16.	2	(3)			46.	3	(41)	*live*
17.	2	(28)	*oldest*		47.	2	(19)	
18.	3	(24)	*sand*		48.	2	(38)	*was named*
19.	2	(37)	*hidden*		49.	1	(50)	*living*
20.	3	(4)			50.	4	(29)	
21.	3	(46)	*particularly*		51.	4	(58)	*make*
22.	1	(59)	*unlike*		52.	2	(42)	*invasion*
23.	3	(47)	*instrumental*		53.	4	(17)	
24.	2	(12)			54.	3	(52)	*a fisherman*
25.	3	(53)	*a*		55.	2	(49)	*in a westerly direction*
26.	2	(20)	*is*		56.	4	(16)	
27.	3	(36)	*will*		57.	2	(56)	*of*
28.	2	(5)			58.	3	(10)	
29.	4	(45)	*their*		59.	3	(51)	*occurring*
30.	3	(25)	*and*		60.	2	(18)	

Post-Test: THE STRUCTURE SECTION

1.	2	(27)	*shorter*		9.	1	(7)	
2.	3	(39)	*stallions*		10.	4	(33)	*gained*
3.	2	(1)			11.	3	(25)	*or*
4.	4	(43)	*them*		12.	3	(6)	
5.	3	(30)	*learned*		13.	4	(23)	*has*
6.	1	(2)			14.	3	(53)	*of an*
7.	3	(31)	*gathered*		15.	2	(34)	*had*
8.	3	(21)	*are*		16.	1	(3)	

17.	4	(60)	*other*
18.	3	(28)	*the largest*
19.	4	(32)	*be used*
20.	3	(4)	
21.	3	(37)	*minted*
22.	2	(55)	*the*
23.	3	(13)	
24.	4	(44)	*their*
25.	1	(35)	*became*
26.	2	(5)	
27.	4	(45)	*its*
28.	2	(56)	*on*
29.	3	(8)	
30.	2	(40)	*number*
31.	2	(24)	*appearance*
32.	2	(12)	
33.	4	(46)	*extremely*
34.	1	(59)	*like*
35.	1	(19)	
36.	3	(20)	*were*
37.	2	(36)	*would*
38.	1	(14)	

39.	3	(47)	*operational*
40.	2	(22)	*Charon were*
41.	3	(15)	
42.	2	(50)	*alone*
43.	3	(54)	*meteorite*
44.	3	(11)	
45.	2	(57)	*extend from*
46.	2	(58)	*made*
47.	4	(16)	
48.	4	(26)	*that of the*
49.	3	(9)	
50.	3	(52)	*a peninsula*
51.	3	(29)	
52.	4	(49)	*in a westerly direction*
53.	2	(51)	*estimated*
54.	1	(10)	
55.	1	(42)	*immigrant*
56.	4	(48)	*the island relentlessly*
57.	2	(17)	
58.	1	(38)	*been admitted*
59.	1	(41)	*fungi*
60.	1	(18)	

TOEFL® COMPUTER-BASED TEST: THE STRUCTURE SECTION

1.	4	(39)	*months*
2.	3	(27)	*shortest*
3.	2	(1)	
4.	3	(60)	*other*
5.	4	(5)	
6.	4	(24)	*mountains*
7.	1	(6)	
8.	1	(22)	*hive are*
9.	2	(12)	
10.	4	(33)	*escapes*

11.	4	(45)	*his*
12.	3	(48)	*almost annihilated*
13.	3	(7)	
14.	3	(58)	*made*
15.	4	(51)	*untreated*
16.	4	(10)	
17.	1	(52)	*the source*
18.	2	(13)	
19.	3	(38)	*was used*
20.	4	(57)	*hailed from*

Answer Key: THE READING SECTION

> The first number following each question number indicates the correct answer to the question. The number in parentheses indicates the skill number (from the *Longman Student CD-ROM*) of the question.

Exercise: MULTIPLE CHOICE QUESTIONS

1. 4 (13)	11. 4 (1)
2. 2 (11)	12. 3 (10)
3. 3 (3)	13. 2 (6)
4. 1 (8)	14. 2 (11)
5. 4 (4)	15. 1 (3)
6. 1 (6)	16. 4 (3)
7. 3 (9)	17. 3 (10)
8. 2 (3)	18. 1 (3)
9. 2 (9)	19. 2 (6)
10. 3 (7)	20. 4 (13)

Exercise: CLICK-ON QUESTIONS

1. *series* (10)	13. P1, S2 (12)
2. P2, S2 (12)	14. B (3)
3. A (3)	15. P1 (1)
4. *the fort* (5)	16. *predator* (10)
5. D (3)	17. *collaborate* (9)
6. P3, S3 (12)	18. *ostrich* (5)
7. *first* (10)	19. *running speed* (5)
8. *Dr. Mudd* (5)	20. *keen* (11)
9. P3 (1)	21. D (3)
10. *sporadic* (10)	22. P3, S6 (12)
11. P4 (1)	23. P3 (1)
12. *beneficial* (9)	

Exercise: INSERTION QUESTIONS

1. A	7. A
2. C	8. E
3. C	9. A
4. C	10. A
5. E	11. C
6. A	

TOEFL® COMPUTER-BASED TEST: THE READING SECTION

1.	1	(3)
2.	4	(6)
3.	*willow bark*	(5)
4.	*characteristics*	(10)
5.	A	(3)
6.	D	(none)
7.	4	(6)
8.	3	(3)
9.	P3, S1	(12)
10.	*prior to*	(9)
11.	3	(11)
12.	2	(2)
13.	3	(10)
14.	4	(4)
15.	*descendents*	(10)
16.	1	(6)
17.	*the name*	(5)
18.	*success*	(10)
19.	*outlived*	(9)
20.	B	(none)
21.	2	(6)
22.	1	(1)
23.	3	(11)
24.	P1, S4	(12)
25.	D	(none)
26.	2	(6)
27.	*destructive*	(9)
28.	3	(11)
29.	C	(3)
30.	*cold front*	(5)
31.	1	(4)
32.	2	(13)
33.	4	(7)
34.	1	(1)
35.	1	(10)
36.	2	(3)
37.	P2, S6	(12)
38.	4	(6)
39.	2	(9)
40.	*acquainted*	(8)
41.	*Captain John Smith*	(5)
42.	4	(3)
43.	*veracity*	(9)
44.	E	(none)

Answer Key: THE WRITING SECTION

EXERCISE 4

1. [L2] [L11] [L18]
2. [L1] [L2] [L11]
3. *For instance* [L4]
4. *Not too long after that...* [L10-11]
5. *it* [L4] = *English* [L3]
6. *it* [L13] = *homework assignment* [L12]
7. *strange response* [L5] = *rather bizarre answer* [L13-14]
8. *"Dunno"* [L6] = *this expression* [L7] = *this mysterious-sounding phrase* [L9] = *a shortened version of "I do not know"* [L9-10]
9. *surprised* [L8] = *amazed* [L13]

EXERCISE 7A

1. I   reasons   missing verb
2. I   Why everyone did not believe   extra subordinate clause connector
3. C   I found
4. I   discusses   missing subject
5. I   preference   missing verb
6. C   piece was found
7. I   How article described   extra subordinate clause connector
8. I   is   missing subject
9. I   agreement   missing verb
10. C   It happened
11. I   Because no one would have made   extra subordinate clause connector
12. I   made   missing subject
13. C   agreement has been reached
14. I   poem   missing verb
15. I   what you told   extra subordinate clause connector
16. C   We forgot
17. I   missing subject and verb
18. I   If you think   extra subordinate clause connector
19. C   decision has been made
20. I   Why you gave   extra subordinate clause connector

EXERCISE 7B

1. I   matter was , I could not decide
2. C   children broke , but parents did not find
3. I   She expected , however she did not graduate
4. C   family moved ; as a result, I had
5. I   I made and I vowed
6. C   Sam did not sign , so he signed
7. C   students waited . Finally, they got
8. I   parents advised he did not take
9. I   job was , later I was given
10. C   Tom wanted , yet he did not know
11. I   We must return , otherwise we will have

12. C   She tries . However, she loses
13. I   Therefore she has gotten , she can pay
14. C   She had ; as a result, she is doing
15. I   They left , it began
16. C   I wanted ; unfortunately, this was
17. C   I will have , or I will not be
18. C   accident happened ; afterwards, police came and wrote
19. I   plan has it has
20. I   directions must be followed , otherwise, outcome will be

EXERCISE 7C

1. I   reason (that he took the money) it was
2. C   (Why that man did something so terrible) will never be known
3. C   ticket (that I needed to get onto the plane) was not included
4. I   (What the lifeguard did) it was
5. I   day (when I found out the news) it was
6. C   teacher (whose advice I remember to this day) was
7. I   (Where we went on vacation) it was
8. I   (That he really said those words) it could not be refuted
9. I   man (who helped me the most in my life) he was
10. C   (How the paper got finished on time) remains
11. I   (What caused the accident on the freeway) it is
12. C   plans (that we made for our trip) were
13. I   process (by which the decisions were made) it was
14. C   (Whatever she gets) is (what she deserves)
15. C   employee (who has the information) (that you need) is
16. I   (What he wrote in the letter) it could not be taken
17. I   officer (who stopped me on the highway) he gave
18. C   (How he could believe something) (that is so incredible) is
19. C   reason (that I applied to the public school) was (that the tuition was lower)
20. I   (Why they said) (what they said to the man) (who tried to help them) it was

EXERCISE 7(A-C)

1.   I definitely believe that taking part in organized team sports is beneficial. However, **it is** beneficial for much more than the obvious reasons. Everyone recognizes, of course, that participation in sports provides obvious physical benefits. It **leads** to improved physical fitness, **and it** also provides a release from the stresses of life. I spent my youth taking part in a number of organized sports, including football, basketball, and volleyball**; as a result of this experience,** I understand that the benefits of this participation go far beyond the physical benefits.

2.   One very valuable benefit that children get from taking part in team **sports is** that it teaches participants teamwork. What any player in a team sport needs to **learn is** that the individual team members must put the team ahead of individual achievement. Individuals on one team who are working for individual glory rather than the good of the **team often** end up working against each other. A team made up of individuals unable to work together often **is not** a very successful team.

3.   What also makes participation in team sports **valuable is** that it teaches participants to work to achieve goals. Playing sports involves setting goals and working toward them; **examples** of such goals are running faster, kicking harder, throwing straighter, or jumping higher. Athletes learn that they can set goals and work toward them until the **goals are** accomplished. **It is** through hard work that goals can be met.

4.   By taking part in sports, **one can learn** the truly valuable skills of working together on teams and working to accomplish specific goals. These skills are not just beneficial in sports; **more importantly,** the skills that are developed through **sports are** the basis of success in many other aspects of life. Mastering these skills **leads** to success not only on the playing field but also in the wider arena of life.

EXERCISE 8A

1.   Recently, some friends and I decided to try a camping trip to get a few days of much-needed relaxation. Only after we had begun this adventure **did we figure out** (17) what a mistake we had made. This experience in the woods **has** (20) taught us that it is better to leave camping either to those who have experience or to those who have a higher degree of tolerance for the surprises of Mother Nature than **do those** (22) of us on this trip.

2.   A few miles from our homes **is a lovely and serene campground** (16), and this seemed like a good place to begin our adventure. As we started out, the picturesque image that we had of camping trips **was** (20) of cute little tents and roaring fires. Our first warning that our trip might not be what we had imagined came when **we tried** (15) to put up our cute little tent. No sooner **had we** (17) begun trying to get the tent up than we learned that this task was not going to be easy. We did finally get the tent up but were unsure of how long **it would** (15) stay up. Then, when trying to build a fire, we discovered that our skill in building fires **was** (20) no better than our skill in raising tents. After a lot more effort, none of the wood **was** (21) burning, so we finally gave up.

3.   Even though we had problems because of our inexperience at camping, we still could have had a reasonable trip **had Mother Nature not** (18) played a few surprises on us. Barely **had the sun** (17) gone down when it started to rain. Feeling rather cold and wet as we huddled in our tent, we started wrapping sleeping bags around ourselves. Suddenly, there **were** (22) several loud shrieks as a snake slithered out of one of the bags. At that point, each one of us **was** (23) completely ready to end our camping adventure. An hour later, when **we were** (15) checking into a motel, we had clearly arrived at the conclusion that camping was not for us. **Were we** (18) to have the opportunity to go camping again, we would in all probability refuse instantly.

EXERCISE 8B

1.   I am still a student, and I have neither started a business **nor** (25) even worked in someone else's company. However, one day when I am **older** (27) and more experienced, it is my dream to have my own business. If I could choose any business to start, I could not choose a **more** (28) satisfying business than a travel agency. A travel agency would allow me not only to share the wonders of my country with others but also **to provide** (25) me with the opportunity to become familiar with the **most pleasant** (27) places in the rest of the world.

2.   My country is beautiful, **appealing** (24), and unique. As a travel agent in my country, it would be my responsibility to familiarize visitors to my country with **the best** (27) that my culture has to offer. This is a responsibility that I would take part in with great pleasure. I would enjoy planning exciting tours for specific interests, such as local cuisine, crafts, or **architecture** (24). I would also offer extended travel packages for visitors who are more interested in relaxing and **enjoying** (24) the natural beauty of my country **than** (27) in rushing around.

3.   Another advantage of owning a travel agency is that it would allow me to become **more knowledgeable** (28) about other places in the world than I currently am. The more educated I am about other places, **the more able I would be** (29) to assist in planning trips outside of my country. I would also have the opportunity as a travel agent to take trips myself and **to see** (24) exciting places with my own eyes. I have read extensively about many places in the world, studied art from many places in the world, and **seen** (24) movies made in other places in the world. I would love to visit the places that I so far know only in books, in studies, and **in movies** (24). It would be my responsibility as a travel agent to learn everything I could about other places, and this, too, seems like the **most wonderful** (27) responsibility.

4.   A travel agency probably would make me neither the richest nor **the most** (25) famous man in the world, but it still seems like an enjoyable and **enriching** (24) company to own. Owning a company that requires me to learn all I can about **the most** (27) exciting places of all within my own country and in other countries of the world would be **more** (27) satisfying to me than **owning** (26) any other type of company.

EXERCISE 8C

1.   The most unexpected event in my life **occurred** (33) on my wedding day, when I was left standing alone at the altar. Prior to this rather memorable day, I **had** (34) fallen in love with a wonderful woman and had **asked** (30) her to become my wife. When she agreed, I thought that I **would** (36) be the happiest man in the world.

2.   On the day of our wedding, however, a big surprise was **waiting** (31) for me. This wonderful fiancée of mine did not show up at the church for the 2:00 ceremony. During that long afternoon, the guests and I **were waiting** (35), patiently at first and then quite impatiently. After more than an hour, I was **convinced** (31) that she had not **shown** (30) up because she **had** (34) decided not to marry me.

3.   I **was** (33) feeling quite devastated, almost suicidal, when suddenly a taxicab pulled up and my bride and her three bridesmaids **were dropped off** (38) in front of the church in rather dirtied gowns. Their car had **broken** (30) down in a deserted area on the way to the church, and they had had to hike for a while until a cab could be **found** (31). After I **recovered** (33) from my shock, the wedding took place.

4.   Even though the shock of standing alone at the altar **was** (33) quite hard for me, I learned a valuable lesson from this experience. I found out just how sad I **would** (36) be to lose this woman, and I **have become** (35) even more thankful since that day to have her with me.

EXERCISE 8D

1.   Humanity has accomplished so **many** (40) great things that it is quite difficult to select one single technological **achievement** (39) as humanity's greatest. To **me** (43), humanity's greatest **achievement** (42) up to now has been the landing on the moon. It represents an extraordinary mixture of successful advanced **technology** (42) and the emotional payback that comes from succeeding at something fantastic.

2.   The **number** (40) of technological requirements for sending a manned spacecraft to the moon, having **it** (45) successfully land on the lunar surface, and allowing humans to climb out of the spacecraft to explore **their** (44) new surroundings was huge. It took a tremendous amount of effort of **many** (40) people working together for incredibly long periods of time under a huge amount of pressure with **little** (40) space for error. A single tiny miscalculation could lead to a **crisis** (41).

3.   Even more important than the technological **success** (42) of the moon landing was the perspective of our home from the moon that this event provided us. This view of the earth from the moon provided every **one** (39) of **us** (43) humans back on earth with a whole new vision of our planet and **its** (45) place in the universe. From our position on earth, it often seems that **we** (43) are at the center of the universe (in spite of how those diagrams in science texts portrayed our solar system and **its** (44) place in the universe). From the moon, though, we could clearly see the Earth in a whole new way. This venture was the **stimulus** (41) for developing an entirely different view of our planet.

EXERCISE 8E

1.   The question of whether it is **preferable** (47) to live in a big city or a small town is one that I have thought about a lot. I have experienced both, I have **an** (53) appreciation of what each type of life has to offer, and I have now developed a **strong preference** (48) for one over the other.

2.   Life in a big city has both benefits and drawbacks. There are **always** (54) **exciting** things to do in the city — places to visit, activities and events to enjoy. However, even though there is so much going on, the city can be **overwhelming** (51) with strangers who are **continuously** (46) rushing around you and without anyone who will share all the city has to offer. Sometimes there are just so many people that you can get lost in a (52) **crowd**. In the city, you can feel **alone** (50) in spite of the fact that you are surrounded by hundreds of thousands of people.

3.   Country life sometimes seems so **boring** (51) — day after day the same people do the same things. The **active life** (48) in the far-off cities, as depicted on television, seems so much more **attractive** (47) than the limited life that surrounds you.

4.   I came from a small village rather than a large city. **The** (55) village where I grew up seemed so dull, and I **eagerly** (46) anticipated finishing high school and heading for a (53) university in a big city. When I first arrived, the city impressed **me tremendously** (48). However, I learned **quickly** (46) that, because people in the city rushed around so much, they did not **have** (52) **time** for each other. People have more time to treat each other **in a friendly way** (49) in a small town, and that is the kind of life that I prefer.

EXERCISE 8F

1.   **In** (56) my first semester at the university, I was overwhelmed by how **unlike** (59) university studies and high school studies were. In high school, I had easily been able to finish the amount of work that was assigned, and if **on** (56) a certain occasion I did not complete an assignment, then the teacher quickly told me to **do** (58) the work. The situation in the university was not at all **like** (59) the situation in high school.

2.   I was greatly **surprised at** (57) the volume of work assigned in the university. **Unlike** (59) high school courses which perhaps covered a chapter in two weeks, university courses regularly covered two or three chapters in one week and two or three **other** (60) chapters the next week. In high school, I had been able to finish the assigned chapters, but in the university it was difficult for me to **keep up with** (57) all the chapters even though I **made** (58) a huge effort.

3.   The role that the teacher took in motivating students to get work done was also very different in the university. In high school, if an assignment was unfinished **on** (56) the date that it was due, my teacher would immediately let me know that I had **made** (58) a mistake and needed to turn **in** (56) the assignment immediately. In the university, however, professors did not **check up on** (57) my work to be sure that I was getting work done regularly. It was quite easy to put **off** (56) studying in the beginning and really have to work hard later to try and **catch up with** (or **to**) (57) the **other** (60) students.

4.   During my first year in the university, I had to **make** (58) a decision to get things done by myself instead of relying **on** (56) **others** (60) to watch over me and ensure that I was doing all that I needed to. With so much more work, this was quite a difficult task to accomplish, but I now regularly try to **do** (58) my best because I **dislike** (59) falling so far behind. It seems that I have turned **into** (56) a pretty motivated student.